Telling the American Story

Telling the American Story
A Structural and Cultural Analysis of Conversational Storytelling

Livia Polanyi

The MIT Press
Cambridge, Massachusetts
London, England

Printed and bound in the United States of America.

Library of Congress Cataloging-in-Publication Data

Polanyi, Livia.
    Telling the American story.

    Bibliography: p.
    Includes indexes.
    1. Discourse analysis, Narrative. 2. Content analysis (Communication) 3. United States--Popular culture. I. Title.
P302.7.P64 1989   401.41   88-13699
ISBN 0-262-66062-8 (pbk.)

Contents

Acknowledgments

We cannot imagine human beings without language, a human society without means for the individual and the collective to remember, recount and restructure past experience, to consider and disseminate the wisdom of the past and the present, and to discuss and explore hopes, fears and plans for the future. It is hard, too, to imagine a culture in which stories of past events told to make a point in a conversation or argument are not often heard. In this book we shall explore the social and cultural constraints which shape the behavior and world view of their tellers through an analysis of the linguistic structure of conversational stories and the social context of their telling.

Undertaking this analysis was an ambitious enterprise which resulted from my own personal encounter with stories and with the power of culture to provide defining contexts for interpreting language and behavior. In the Afterword, I will discuss those encounters at some length. In this Preface then, I should like to name those who have most deeply influenced both the ideas in this book and their rather unorthodox presentation.

The influence of Erving Goffman and Gregory Bateson—both of whom I was privileged to have met—is most strongly felt in these pages. Above anyone else, they brought home to me both the painful near impossibility and hopeful, brave necessity for the individual to BE and to DO in a world of constantly conflicting and often paradoxical social and cultural forces. Directly relevant to the subject matter of the book is William Labov's analysis of oral narrative and the work on the nature and mechanics of conversational interaction done by the late Harvey Sacks and his colleagues. Their work forms the basis of the microanalysis of conversational stories in Chapters 2 and 3 of this book.

In addition I would like to name Professors Pete Becker and Vern Carroll, who introduced me to the work of these scholars and whose own approaches to the complexities of language, culture and scholarship have left a lasting impression on me and on this book. And most especially, I would like to thank András Kornai, Remko Scha, Nicolás Wey and Ellen Zweig whose practical help and constant support over many years has resulted in this new edition of *Telling the American Story*.

Telling the American Story

1

Stories as Cultural Texts (Not All Stories Are American Stories)

1.0 Introduction: American Stories

The title of this book, *The American Story*, is a pun. In the discussion which follows, stories from ordinary conversations provide material from which cultural primitives of a more general American Cultural Story are derived.

The stories which will be analyzed in this book are "normal," "acceptable," "understandable" commonplace productions.[1] They are "about" normal events and make unremarkable "points" in their telling. In order to explore what these stories really are about, and to relate the "points" they make to general matters of concern in American culture, we will adopt a radically different methodology from other approaches taken to determine what texts are about.

This question of determining what a text is "about" is far from simple. Most analyses of stories are content analyses of one sort or another. In such an analysis, a story is approached by saying "Well, this, and this and that are all mentioned in the story and therefore the story must be "about" this and this and that." Stories are

---

[1] I do not believe that the method of cultural analysis which I am proposing here is, by any means, the only way to reach cultural primitives. As contemporary anthropology makes clear, there are many. However, I do believe that an associative expansion of the obvious is one important method. Similarly, while many source texts can provide insight into a culture, I believe that conversational stories and tales are one widely available access route to folk truths and values.

composed of many "thisses and thats," however. They are made up of numerous events and states of affairs involving numerous characters and situations. Content analyses of all sorts have failed to justify precisely why some "thisses and thats" are what the story is "about" and others are not.

A determination of what is important, what is seized upon as important, is made not by naming elements themselves, but by understanding the importance of those elements to the point which the teller is making in telling the story. Tellers are very aware of the need to separate out more salient information from less salient information as they are recounting their stories. They display great sensitivity in assigning different weights to the different propositions in the storyworld through the rhetorical markings assigned to each one. Therefore, in this study, a methodology is presented which begins with transcripts of conversational stories and produces a paraphrase of the story as told by means of careful attention to the details of encoding the various propositions about what went on when and why in the storyworld. This paraphrase consists only of those elements which the teller most heavily foregrounded in the telling. Such a paraphrase, which can be used in investigations of all sorts, from narrative analysis to psycholinguistic studies of memory, is used in the present case as an object for cultural analysis.

In the fourth chapter of this book, "The World Evoked by American Stories," the propositions composing the paraphrase of the conversational stories discussed in the earlier chapters are expanded into a discussion of basic American values and beliefs. This expansion is done by asking what is most interesting, storyworthy, or compelling about the elements in the propositions themselves.[2] The presuppositions structuring the expansion text are

_____

2 An analyst wishing to examine the stories of a culture not his own using the linguistic methodology presented here would need to make use of a cultural initiate to expand the story propositions into a "thick text," (Geertz, 1973) precisely as a linguist investigating the grammar of a language other than his own must make use of a native speaker informant to make the

themselves then distilled and organized into an abstract American Cultural Grammar. This, in its turn, is used in the last chapter to produce a generic American Story consisting of "Basic Truths" about the nature of the world and the proper conduct of human relationships. This study can be considered a generative cultural exegesis in which texts are produced from other texts, expanded, distilled into their elements, which are themselves expanded into a text to be subjected to the same processes of abstraction into elementary propositions.

In expanding the propositions in the stories themselves (which were, with one exception, told in undirected conversations among American born, English speaking, white, middle class friends) I have used myself, a reasonably acculturated native-born American, as an informant. In doing so, I was operating within the tradition of transformational grammarians who have long used their own "native speaker intuitions" as a source of insight into the syntactic acceptability of sentences in their own languages. My ordinary judgments are correct insofar as the resulting text seems a string of clichés to my compatriots. Insofar as another cultural American finds himself surprised by an observation, I have failed to capture the "unintentionally obvious." These self-evident "everyone knows this" truths differ tremendously from culture to culture. Because we always base our linguistic texts upon these implicitly assumed notions, genuine, satisfactory cross-cultural communication is most unlikely if, indeed, it is possible at all. This book, therefore, will, like all other texts, be one sort of "story" for those who share my cultural presuppositions (if not my scientific standpoint) and it must necessarily be quite another text for those who do not. This does not mean that we cannot profit enormously from interactions with those different from ourselves—lest this be taken as a plea for

---

important grammaticality decisions. Otherwise, the would-be analyst is likely to build up a composite picture of what would have been interesting about the story materials had the analyst told stories in which they figured prominently and would surely miss almost entirely the impact of the various goings-on in the storyworld on the teller and others who share the teller's world view.

xenophobia—but we must accept that the interaction we are having with them is necessarily different from the interaction they are having with us, even with the best will in the world.

1.1 American Texts and American Values

This book, written by an American, is, itself, an American text which consistently reveals the cultural origin of its producer. The choice of subject, the nature of the argumentation, the tone and style of its presentation, even this self-reflexive meta-comment, all declare it to be an American text—perhaps more insistently to one who is not an American than to someone who is. Rather than treat this book as autonomous and anonymous, I will sometimes intrude upon the discourse. While this is unusual in scientific discussions, I cannot justify separating myself from the analysis which necessarily resulted in large part from my own Americanness. A stance of scientific impersonality, while surely more comfortable in many ways than the unconventional stance adopted here, weakens a cultural exploration, especially of one's own culture, because it deprives those who wish to understand the analytic process of much valuable data which could be used in constructing models of the target culture.

1.1.1 An American Story
Having said this, then, I would now like to share some of the experiences which have brought home to me, in the years since completing the research on which this book is based, how American I really am, how a part of one's formative culture every human being ultimately is, and how decisive a role cultural conditioning plays in the construction and interpretation of linguistic and behavioral texts.

The data on which this book is based came from hours of tape-recorded conversations of my friends talking casually at dinner, in the evening after a party, to one another, and to me. I found it relatively easy to ask them if I might make use of our social interactions for my work. That my work was almost always on my mind seemed natural for me and for them, and they had no difficulty granting me permission to tape them freely. Yes, of course, they wanted to see exactly which texts I would pick to analyze and were often curious to read what I wrote about them, but they did not feel I was acting inappropriately in "working" as we were visiting with one another. In many other cultures, even in Western European countries which seem to resemble North America in many ways, such a redefinition of a social situation into a "work" situation would not be possible even among serious-minded academics with similar interests and background. In Holland, for example, where I lived and worked for several years, to "use" one's friends for research and analysis would be viewed by most academics as a violation of the social contract. It would be considered a thoughtless, selfish act in which one person put one's own personal wants and needs above the well-being of others.

Of course, like any expatriate, I would tell endless stories of misunderstandings and difficulties I had trying to adjust to living and working Someplace Else, even an Else as comfortable, as affluent, as modern, and as genuinely decent as The Netherlands. But I will restrain myself and tell only one story which describes the experience through which I became aware of the differences between Dutch and American attitudes towards the role which *work* should properly play in one's life and in one's discourse.

After I had been in Holland for a while, I noticed that something odd happened in a conversation when I was asked how I had come to find myself there more or less permanently. At first, I had treated this question as more or less unproblematic. I would explain that I was there because of my job. Basically, I would say, I had acquired my job through an ad in an American professional journal asking for someone with my qualifications. Needing a job, and intrigued by the promise of an interview in Amsterdam, I answered the ad, was interviewed in Holland, and was hired on the spot. So, I ended up moving to Holland and had been there since. I would then be quite confused when my questioner would persist in asking me again why I had come to Holland. Patiently, I would explain that the job was suited to my interests and that I had a chance to teach and do research in my particular specializations. "Oh," I would hear, and the conversation would immediately shift to some very natural or business-related topic and I would feel a definite sense of disappointment and distance emanating from my interlocutors.

After having had this experience a number of times over a couple of years, I finally asked some native informants what was going on. Why had they found my answer so bewildering, so off-putting? Since they were students in my seminar on Dutch and American cultural values, where this sort of question was more or less appropriate, they explained, after looking at each other nervously for a while, that they really had wanted to know why I had come. They then explained that they had felt a bit let down and betrayed by my answer; they had considered their daring to ask the question at all a sign of their willingness to accept the offer of relative intimacy and informality which my American classroom manner promised. When I had given an answer telling them only about my work, they felt as if I had rejected them, refusing to give an honest answer. "After all," they said, "there must be a *real* reason why you left America and chose to come here." When I asked what sort of "real" reason they had in mind, they suggested that perhaps I liked the political situation or cultural atmosphere in Europe better than that in the United States, or perhaps I thought that Holland was more beautiful than America.

We discussed their expectations and my answer for quite a while, and gradually it became clear that what I had given as (conventional) valid reasons for an important life decision struck them as evasive and irrelevant, "not real." And on my part, and from what I find an unexceptional American perspective, it would never have occurred to me that answers which would ring true in Holland would involve my personal life only and neither professional nor intellectual considerations. After a bit more exploration, it became clear that another reason which would have been quite acceptable might have involved money; had the job in

Holland paid better than one in the United States I could have used the financial reason without further explanation.

The reasons I had given, however, all related to my "work," were almost incomprehensible. How could anyone leave friends, family and home behind to come to Holland only for "work"? And if it were really the case that I had done so, how could I possibly admit so casually, so callously, to being "ambitious" (which is very, very badly thought of in Holland). And not only ambitious, but a *vakidioot* to boot. (*Vakidioot* is the sort of untranslatable word which always appears in anecdotes of this kind. It can be glossed as "a one-sided academic grind who is interested only in his field.") Who would willingly present herself as a *vakidioot*—someone poorly socialized, boring, and selfish, who thinks and talks about only what she is interested in and does not take into account the fact that other people may be bored by her work? In Holland, the presupposition is that people are only interested in what *they* know and are therefore obviously bored by someone else's field. It is rude to discuss a subject with which you are extremely familiar with people who know little about it. It is considered polite to talk about only common rather than "specialized" subjects in a social situation, even with colleagues, while to talk about a work-related interest would seem very one-sided and rude.

So, my conventional, impersonal, unimpeachable American explanation of why I went to Holland was, for my Dutch hosts, completely unconventional, potentially overly-revealing and socially incomprehensible. While I was giving an explanation which presented a self which was rational, sensible, businesslike, work-oriented, committed and serious, they were hearing about a self which was cold, calculating, uncaring, work-obsessed, ambitious, and slightly inhuman. They could only believe that I was rejecting their attempts at intimacy by giving them a story which could not possibly be believed, thereby signalling them that they were coming too close in asking me a personal question. The alternative, even more disturbing, was that I was showing much more of my "true self" than was appropriate, that they had come too close to someone no reasonable Dutch person would want to be associated with.

This is one of the (unfortunately) endless examples of bungled cross-cultural communications I might have chosen. In telling this story I am *not* claiming that Dutch and American people necessarily do things for different reasons (which they may well do, but that is properly the subject of a separate investigation). I am claiming, however, that the *reasons* which are acceptable to give in explaining or justifying one's actions are often different among the two peoples. Dutch discourse is sufficiently different from American discourse so that a "normal" story in one culture is often not a "normal" story in the other. Just as jokes seldom travel well, the everyday conversational story, commonplace justification, argument, or explanation is often (unpredictably) less successful abroad than at home. Attempting to find out how the same text might be interpreted by members of two different cultures can lead an analyst quite far afield from the original text. Just now, we have needed to trace the connotations of words and chase up and down the paths of cultural reasoning to explain what was going on in the cross-cultural "communication breakdown" described above. In other words, in order to make sense out of everyday conversational texts, one ends up engaged in the entire anthropological enterprise of figuring out what a set of texts in a given culture "means" and how that meaning is communicated through the structure of the texts.

1.1.2 Why Not Consult the Experts?
In this book, we try to answer a number of questions. For example:

What do Americans think the world is like?
What are people like: How should people behave?
What is important?
What is unimportant?
How are adults different from children?
Are adults different from children?
How is the world organized or is it organized?
How do we know what we know?
How de we select what is worth knowing?
Why do we think that knowing is important at all? etc.

Since a great deal has been written by psychologists, sociologists, and anthropologists about these matters, why not use stories speakers tell as data and then use the experts' "objective" analyses as the basis for discussion? Well, a close examination of what the "experts" tell us reveals that their observations and arguments are built on exactly the sorts of presupposed information we are actually trying to discover: ideas about what the world is like, how people are supposed to behave, what they are supposed to want and need, and all the rest.

My purpose here is not to attack the experts for not being *objective*: the very need for objectivity is, in itself, one of the ideas which will be examined. Rather, my starting point will be to admit this lack of objectivity, and explore our reliance on *objectivity* and *truth* as an entry into the network of beliefs, attitudes and commonly held understandings which constitute American life.

Let us now look briefly at only one example from social science literature, drawn almost at random, and examine briefly how culturally salient presuppositions are present as strongly in "scientific" explanations of the social world as in that observed world itself. These paragraphs are excerpted from a sociological account of contemporary working-class family life, *Worlds of Pain: Life in the Working Class Family* (L. Breslow Rubin: 1976).

In other ways, too, the realities of class make themselves felt both inside and outside the home. The professional man almost invariably is more highly educated than his wife—a fact that gives him an edge of superiority in their relationship; not so with his working-class counterpart. The professional man has the prospect of a secure and orderly work life—his feet on a prestigious and high-salaried career ladder; not so with his working-class counterpart. The professional man is a respected member of the community outside his home—his advice sought, his words valued; not so with his working-class counterpart.

Thus, the professional middle-class man is more secure, has more status and prestige than the working-class man—factors which enable him to assume a less *overtly* authoritarian role within the family. There are, after all, other places, other situations where his authority and power are tested and accorded legitimacy. At the same time, the demands of his work role for a satellite wife require that he risk the consequences of the more egalitarian family ideology. In contrast, for the working-class man, there are few such rewards in the world outside the home; the family usually is the only place where he can exercise power, demand obedience to his authority. Since his work role makes no demands for wifely participation, he is under fewer and less immediate external pressures to accept the *egalitarian ideology*. (p. 99) [emphasis in original]

Let's not try to track down every presupposition in these paragraphs, but merely point out a few which will emerge later in the book.

Beginning at the beginning, there is a statement that "realities of class make themselves felt" which is predicated on the self-evident truth (to the writer and audience) that there is such a thing as *reality* and furthermore that one can know something about it. Once there is a construct of *reality* one supposes that there would be a concept we could loosely call *non-reality* and indeed, there are a variety of *non-realities* including illusions, dreams, fantasies, lies and delusions. One American task is to separate out the *real* from the *unreal*, the *true* from the *false*. An adult who could not do so would be, in our eyes, a somewhat less than adequate person.

Continuing to the next sentence, we learn that the professional man's education puts him at an advantage in his relationship with his wife. Why, we might ask, is the *fact* of having a better education something which gives one an advantage? And furthermore, we might ask what a *fact* is and what it means to have an *advantage in a relationship*? Understanding this sentence is based on the reader and writer accepting a set of presuppositions about the relationship between *knowledge* and *power* and how *power* is manifest in human interactions: what is important about it, why anyone would think to investigate it.

Continuing through these paragraphs is a set of assumptions about the importance of having power to an individual and the belief that being powerless in one sphere of life must be made up for by the exercise of power in another arena. Since the working man has few satisfactions (*rewards*) for his *need* for authority and power on the job, he will have to find them in the home. Therefore, reader and writer must both accept that *power* exists, that there is a need for it, and that life can be looked at as a sort of ledger sheet where one kind of experience can make up for another. Thus there is *life* and there is something apart from life which is also important and relevant—an abstract system of *needing* and *wanting* which can be *satisfied* apart from the time and place in which a lack is felt.

This relates to another sentence in this text, and the last one we will look at, which assumes that there can be a distinction between the way an individual *acts* and the way he really *is*. What does it imply about the beliefs of reader and writer to say that "[certain] factors. . . enable the professional man to assume a less overtly authoritarian role"? Clearly, the author is maintaining that the professional father is authoritarian although he acts as if he were not authoritarian. Whether one accepts this analysis or not is beside the point; what is important is that an American reader has no trouble believing that one can act differently from the way one truly is, and that, in fact, *things are often not what they seem*. In other words, the world appears to be one way and may actually be quite different if we only know what it is really like.

1.1.3 Why Do This Analysis At All?
And what is the world really like? What are Americans really like? Clearly, we address these questions because we too share the attitude that it is important to know what is *really* happening, and that it is a worthwhile and not *unrealistic* enterprise to examine cultural phenomena in order to *get beneath the surface* of them and understand more about reality than appears on the surface. As such, this is in itself a cultural text, and, indeed, any utterance by any speaker anywhere is based on culturally significant presuppositions about what is worth talking about, or needs to be talked about, or should be talked about in a given context, as well as more complex issues of content which we have been looking at briefly above.

Since each utterance, and especially each discourse (a loosely defined term which we will use here to mean something which will probably be longer than one clause which functions as a unit in a linguistic exchange) is a potential cultural text which contains within it material which could be drawn out for cultural analysis, one task of the linguist interested in how speakers actually use language is to develop methods of looking at linguistically realized texts to see how that culturally salient material is encoded.

1.2 A note about "Americans"

Conversational stories are highly structured linguistic productions. The information conventionally included in storytellings is organized in highly predictable ways, as shall be discussed at length in subsequent chapters. However, before going on to technical discussions of narrative structure, it is important to consider the nature of the "Americans" included within the scope of the claims about story structure, conversational behavior, and world view presented in this book.

I am an educated, middle class, white, adult woman. Most of the tellers of the stories in this book are women of similar background. A number, too, are "East Coast Jews" who share with me a number of stylistic conversational characteristics of the type discussed by Tannen (1984). All tellers have English as a first language and none have strong ties outside of "mainstream" Middle-American society, except for the adolescent narrator of "The Baddest Girl in the Neighborhood," who is a member of the Philadelphia inner city Black community.[3]

In gathering stories for this book, I did not attempt to find a cross-section of speakers. All of the tellers, as it turns out, are Northerners, all are urban or suburban dwellers, and all but one are adults who are reasonably well-off financially—although none are extremely well-to-do. Although we do not deal with the influence of race, class, sex, age, or other social factors in storytelling, this does not mean that I do not appreciate their importance in shaping linguistic productions or life experience. American society is far from homogeneous, of course, and there are very different norms of

---

[3] This story was collected by W. Labov and is used here with his permission.

behavior and strong differences of opinion about style of life and the relative importance of some values over others among different segments of American society. However, in this study I examine only those aspects of American life and thought which are basic to being a socialized, reasonably acculturated person in America.

These values underlie political slogans and lie below the surface in advertising campaigns. They persuade Americans of all races, classes, and educational levels to support candidates, to desire, to buy. Those values are in *Ebony* and *Jet* no less than in *Time*, *Newsweek*, or *The Ladies' Home Journal*. They determine the very issues around which the Black Civil Rights Movement has rallied and informs the rhetoric of the other "mainstream" minority groups in their American demands for "fairness," "justice," "opportunity," "equality" and "freedom." Most assimilated, English speaking, Asian Americans, Gay Americans, Handicapped Americans, Jewish Americans and Female Americans as well as Black Americans and Nonminority Americans accept without question that these "rights" constitute "equality" and "freedom" which are themselves the prerequisites for the "satisfying," "decent" and, above all, "happy" life which each "individual" deserves without question.[4]

From an "insider's" point of view, the social world is composed of distinct subgroups distinguished from one another by clearly relevant criteria such as position, property, customs or beliefs. The outsider, however, does not distinguish one group of insiders from another. The similarities among the Others outweigh and obscure

---

[4] Native Americans, unassimilated foreign born, or non-English speaking ethnic minorities as well as some historically isolated rural or religious groups might not accept this complex of assumptions as automatically. They may have alternative world views which allow them to make a very different sort of sense out of their experience than their "American" neighbors. These residents and citizens of the United States are outside of the American "mainstream." They are different, foreign, exotic.

These "exotic" minorities may well see no significant differences among those outside their own group. The "Others" may all be "Americans," "Whitemen," "City Folks," or "Nonbelievers." Those of us within mainstream American society, on the other hand, see many very distinct groups separated from one another and from "our" group by a myriad salient characteristics.

the possible differences, reducing them in the end to insignificance (Lotman, 1978). Let me give one brief example out of my own experience to illustrate Lotman's point.

My students in Amsterdam insisted that it is impossible to make any generalizations about "Dutch" culture at all. (They *all* insisted as well that making any sort of generalization is wrong.) After all, they said, the various regions of The Netherlands are so different from one another. To be correct, we should talk about rural Dutch culture versus urban Dutch culture (and Amsterdam versus Rotterdam versus the rest of the country). In addition, we must distinguish between "middle class Dutch culture" and "working class Dutch culture" and, of course, "Northern Calvinist Dutch culture" and "Southern (easygoing) Dutch culture." As an outsider in the country, however, I saw only the very slightest differences among these groups. For me, the Dutch are one very homogeneous cultural entity. However, I find Americans from the East Coast very different from Americans from the West Coast and Americans from the Midwest very different from Americans from either Coast. Black Americans seem very different from White Americans and university-educated Americans very different from Americans with little formal schooling. I find great differences as well between male Americans and female Americans. For my Dutch friends, colleagues and students we are all very much alike. When I asked my students what they found so similar among us all, they tended to get a bit embarrassed and finally replied, in what seemed to me a very blunt Dutch way, *"You know!* You're all so incredibly *American."*

2

The Structure of Stories

2.0 Introduction

Competent users of language recognize when a story is being told. In an American conversation, story recipients are alerted by conventional story introducers which a would-be storyteller uses to signal the intention to tell a story. The talk then moves out of the here and now of the conversation into a storyworld: another time, often another location, populated by other participants. The teller makes use of deictic markers in a way which indicates a change of frame of reference and no one is surprised if the narrator speaks from a perspective not his own. All these world-building and world-populating activities are familiar from innumerable other story-tellings. As the telling unfolds, there is a clear expectation that "what happened" in that other time and place will become clear.

In this chapter, the nature of stories in general is explored and the linguistic realization of stories in English is specified in some detail. This work builds on the work done by William Labov, both in his 1967 paper with Joshua Waletsky, "Narrative Syntax," and in his 1972 paper, "The Transformation of Experience in Narrative Syntax," from the book, *Language in the Inner City.* The discussion provides a methodology for abstracting from the surface structure of a text those propositions about the storyworld which, if taken together, are the essence of the story as told. The significance of the presuppositions upon which these propositions are built to Americans in general will be explored in the concluding sections of this book.

2.1 Narratives and Events

Narrative discourse models the passage of time in some *world* by building up a *time line* demarcated by discrete moments at which instantaneous occurrences are reported to take place. There are various forms of *narrative* which can be thought of as describing the states of affairs obtaining in different types of worlds. In this book we shall be analyzing examples of one form of narrative, the *story*, which differs from other types of narrative because in recounting a story, a teller describes events which took place in one specific past time world in order to make some sort of *point* about the world which teller and story recipients share. Other types of narratives differ from stories along dimensions of time, specificity of world described, and the necessity for the teller to make a recognizable point in the telling. *Plans* and *simultaneous narrations* describe events in non-past worlds while *generic narratives* detail what usually or always occurs in worlds of a certain sort rather than what did happen in one specific world on one specific occasion. Plans, simultaneous narrations and generic narratives are all forms of *report* in which the teller need not be making a specific point in his exposition but may merely be recounting past, present or future events. Unlike the story teller, the reporter relies on the listener and the context of telling to supply the point of the telling.[1]

In any narrative, some of the events form the *main time line*—a series of successive instants in the narrated world which correspond to the moving reference point in the narrative construction of that world. *Event* is used here to mean an occurrence in some world which is described as having an instantaneous rather than a durative or iterative character. In the world's languages, there are various means available to indicate events. In the Indo-European languages,

---

1   Although all the narratives we shall be concerned with will be linguistic texts, narratives are not necessarily linguistically encoded. Narrative films and plays, as well as narrative paintings, music and dance, and narrative poems and jokes are built around a series of events marking the progress of time in the world conjured up by the piece.

including English, this semantic information is carried by the aspectual component of the tense-carrying verb in a clause. Those events syntactically encoded in main clauses form the main time line. *Event clauses* are semantically *noniterative, non-habitual* and *temporarily bounded* (Labov and Waletsky 1967; Vendler 1967; Labov 1972; Hopper and Thompson 1980; Polanyi 1978, 1985; Kamp and Rohrer 1982; Hinrichs 1981, 1986; Dowty 1986, etc). In non-Indo-European languages, according to Jones and Jones (1979), and Hopper and Thompson (1980), the distinction between main line event clauses and other clauses may be made with narrative particles or by special morphological marking somewhere on the clause.[2]

Narrative texts are seldom composed only of event clauses, however, but contain stative clauses as well which differ from event clauses in temporal interpretation. Such *state clauses* encode states of affairs which persist over some interval of time in the discourse world rather than occurring at one unique discrete instant.

2.2 Narrative Genres

Stories and *past time reports* are *specific, affirmative, past time narratives which tell about a series of events which took place at specific unique moments in a unique past time world.* The narrative line in these discourse genres in English is built with simple past tense event clauses or with a combination of these clearly past time clauses and

---

2   When the event clauses in narrative texts are abstracted out, however, it is clear that not all event clauses necessarily participate in the narrative "main line" by advancing the temporal reference point. Some event propositions may be interpreted at the same moment or even at a time point previous to events which precede them in the text (Nerbonne, 1986).

In "Keeping It All Straight: Interpreting Narrative Time in Real Discourse," (Polanyi, 1987) we show how a set of independent counter-examples to the basic narrative generalization that event clauses mark strict temporal progression (these include "flashbacks," "repairs" and "true starts" [see Chapter 3 below]) can be resolved in terms of *embedded discourse structures* which interrupt the development of an ongoing narrative unit by introducing propositions requiring interpretation relative to timelines in possible worlds other than those in which the propositions of the developing narrative obtain. A POP or legal return to continue the interrupted narrative occurs only when licensed by general rules of discourse formation.

morphologically present tense clauses which are given a past time semantic interpretation (the so-called "historical present tense"). The events are specific and affirmative. Event clauses may use transitive or intransitive verbs and tend to have specific agents and, if transitive, objects.[3]

Narrative discourses never include more than one distinct event proposition. There is no limit on the number of state propositions which may legitimately be part of a narrative. States in narratives may come into being at a particular moment and last until a specific time while events in the discourse may act as beginning or end points for the interval of time for which the state obtains. Other states begin or end gradually during a period bracketed by events, while still others end slowly and at an indefinite, unspecified time. States may obtain for a whole narrative or only for the shortest possible interval of time.

---

3   However, in a generic narrative, any given event, agent, or object is not unique, but stands for a class of such events, agents, or objects, since the world of the narration is not a unique world, but is rather a class of worlds in which the activities and circumstances described generally obtain. Generic past time narratives are structured around indefinite past time events encoded in event clauses with generic modals such as *would* or *used to* (Joos, 1968). The meaning of an event in a generic past time narrative could be glossed as "It would *always* be the case that at this exact moment in the proceedings, 'Event X took place.'"

Similarly, the meaning of an event clause in a generic present time narrative can be glossed 'Always,' at this exact moment in the proceedings, 'Event X takes place.' This is quite distinct from the semantic interpretation accorded a main line event clause in a simultaneous narration: "At this exact moment in both the narrative world and the world of the narration, 'Event X is taking place.'" Although the two "present tense" clauses may be morphologically identical, they are accorded very different interpretations due to clues elsewhere in the discourse.

Plans and other descriptions of wished for but yet unrealized sequences of events and negative narratives which describe a sequence of occurrences which did not or ought not to occur are encoded in event clauses with modal markers indicating the type of assertion being made. Remote past events in otherwise past time narrative genres are often in the pluperfect, although if there are a series of such events, each one need not be so marked. Similarly, in a present time narration, a simple past tense event will establish a time line previous to the moment of time in the embedding discourse. In all cases, however, the clauses capable of initiating or continuing a discrete time line are punctual, noniterative, and completive.

Some states obtain in the world of narrating as well as in the world created through the narration; some obtain at all times in all worlds, while others may be less universal in scope.

Conventions of narration, in English, at least, call for universally true propositions to occur early in a telling, followed by more restricted state propositions, followed by a section of event clauses and states restricted to intervals of time in the narrative world. Time in narratives funnels in towards the NOW of the narrative genre (towards past time events, in past time narratives; towards the moment of speaking in simultaneous narrations; towards the specific future instants when events are to occur in plans, etc.) As Grimes (1982) has shown in his analysis of "The Gettysburg Address," even nonnarrative discourses may be organized as a temporal progression from the universally true, through those states and events which preceded the moment of narrative center (the RIGHT NOW of the moment the speech was delivered), through to a (possibly indefinite) future time. Unless marked as being "out of place" by some sort of comment or displacement phenomenon (such as the *true start* discussed in Polanyi, 1978b, and in Chapter 3) deviations from this order are used to signal a new *episode* in the narrative, one with different temporal, spatial, or personal deictic anchoring.

As we begin to look at stories in some detail a bit further on, it will become increasingly clear that speakers adhere very consistently to the narrative conventions outlined here. There is nothing structurally "casual" about an everyday story. Upon close examination, a story told in a conversation reveals itself to be as formally constructed as any carefully worked out acknowledged piece of literary verbal art. Just as a conventional novelist will take pains to make clear where a story took place geographically and temporally, who was involved, and what important events had happened previous to the beginning of the story he wants to tell, a conversational storyteller telling a casual friend what went on the supermarket checkout line last Wednesday will supply enough relevant setting information to locate the story in time and space early on in the telling. Throughout the story, information important to understanding the state of affairs in the storyworld will be given at times appropriate to building and updating an adequate model of the changing world of the discourse.

To distinguish those propositions encoding states of affairs in a narrative world which are not punctual events on the main time line from those events which are, we shall refer to the state and non-main line events collectively as *durative-descriptive propositions*. These are encoded in *durative-descriptive clauses*. Descriptions of characters, settings, and motivations are durative-descriptive, along with habitual, iterative, or noninstantaneous actions and events which are semantically interpreted to be off the main time line, in flash sequences, for example. In stories and reports, the narative genres discussed in this study, durative-descriptive clauses often predominate.

2.3 Stories: Specific Past Time Narratives with a Point

Linguistic texts are produced to accomplish communicative aims. *Stories* are told to make a point, to transmit a message—often some sort of moral evaluation or implied critical judgment—about the world the teller shares with other people. Exactly what telling a story involves in this respect, can be gotten at somewhat indirectly by considering the *report*, often linguistically identical to the story in terms of event and state information, but differing dramatically in impact. Any parent who has ever received a dreary *report* of the day's happenings instead of a *story* in response to a cheery "Well, dear, what happened in school today?" will testify to the difference.

A *report*, unlike a *story*, is most typically elicited by the recipient—like the hapless parent in the example above—or in response to circumstances which require an accounting of what went on. The context of reporting supplies a framework in which the relevance of the states and events reported can be ascertained. In fact, the recipient may even assign relevance to very specific pieces of information whose importance escapes the narrator, as in reports by witnesses to the police. The burden of assigning differential weighting to the various narrated propositions thus falls on the receiver of the report. The reporter himself may implicitly tell the elicitor, "O. K., you wanted to know. *You* figure out why I should have told you all this." In a story, however, key events bring about changes in the storyworld which are relevant to the point which is being made, while less important events move people and objects about and mark the passage of time necessary to a narrative. Likewise, some crucial durative-descriptive information communicates those states of affairs which are altered by the key events. Other durative-descriptive propositions are properly considered "background" information. Tellers, therefore, *evaluate* key events most highly in order to distinguish them from other less important instantaneous main time line events (Labov and Waletsky, 1967; Labov, 1972). Crucial durative-descriptive information is likewise highlighted by the teller in the telling to emphasize the most important non-event story propositions. Evaluation allows the story recipients to build up a model of the relevant information in the text which matches the teller's intentions as signalled by the manner in which the informaiton about the storyworld is communicated.

2.3.1 Evaluation in Conversational Stories

In storytelling, the burden of making the relevance of the telling clear falls on the narrator. Insofar as they share a common world view, the narrator and intended story recipients have similar basic understanding of people, objects, and occurrences—the material world, in short, and the intricate complex of values and beliefs which are used to assign meaning to the goings-on in that world and to make sense of experience. The narrator relies upon this common understanding to constrain the interlocutors to infer the same point from the goings on in the story worlds which he himself infers. Although the narrator may make the message of the story explicit in an introductory comment or concluding remark, the juxtaposition of events and states which make up the telling must be encoded so that the message is clear even without those added remarks.

Stories are highly complex discourses, however, and not all the propositions about the storyworld are equally important to the point which the story is being told to illustrate. In essence, a story consists of events which took place in particular circumstances, involved particular characters, and gave rise to states of affairs which contrast in some way with the situation obtaining in the storyworld at the beginning of the story. Every world is composed of innumerable states of affairs, and a storyworld is no different. However, only a few of these are significant to the point being made in a given telling and, therefore, only the events which cause altertions in those states bring about a contrasting state which is "meaningful."

In telling a story, the narrator has two tasks: to give enough detail so that interlocutors understand the nature of the change brought about, and to differentiate among the various events and states which are used to tell the story so that it is clear to the listeners precisely which complex of circumstances and events should be used to infer the point being made. Highlighting the most important information in the story at the expense of less important information is accomplished by according each proposition a more or less distinctive form of encoding; the more distinct the encoding, the more the information encoded stands out from the rest of the text and the better it is remembered. Put most generally, the more salient the form of encoding, the more salient the information encoded is assumed to be.

Evaluation, as this process of assigning prominence is called, is accomplished by encoding the information to be accorded increased weight in a way which departs from the local norm of the text. In spoken language, speakers signal salience by using any one of a fairly large battery of conventional linguistic and paralinguistic *evaluative devices* drawn from every level of linguistic structure (Labov, 1972). It should be borne in mind, however, that there are no "absolute" evaluative devices; any device available for evaluation can be used nonevaluatively as well or can be so over-used that it becomes a textual norm.

Phonologically, a speaker may pronounce a word in a distinctive way, accentuate an odd syllable, or use a distinctive dialectal sound quality. Changes in stress and volume are also available to mark prominence as well as onomatopoeia, rhyme, and nonlinguistic noises. Lexically, a speaker may choose a word from a different register from the text norm—perhaps using a colloquial word in a formal text or vice-versa; "loaded" words may be used and words rich in connotation. Profanity, foreign words and precise use of relatively infrequent words also can be used to draw attention to the proposition so encoded.

Syntactically, as Labov (1972) has shown, a multitude of resources are available, including modification, the use of comparators, superlatives, and negative sentences (which evaluate what *was* the state of affairs in the storyworld by making explicit what was not the case). Modal operators and adverbials which shift the point of view from one frame of reference to another can also be evaluative, as can other types of elaboration and specification phenomena which highlight some aspect of the discourse world by giving a good deal of information about it. Any marked change in syntactic complexity calls attention to itself whether by a shift into a simple sentence from a stretch of hightly attenuated sentences or vice versa. In stories, the first event after a string of durative-descriptive clauses demands special attention, as does the first complex sentence after a number of relatively short uncomplicated sentences.

At the discourse level, a wide variety of devices are available; repetition, reported speech or thought, flashbacks or flashaheads which delay the action, and explicit meta-comments as well as "clustering" a number of events at the "peak" of the story are common in many narrative traditions around the world (Longacre,1976). While "reported speech and thought" is often an important discourse level evaluative device, it should be pointed out that direct and indirect discourse only function evaluatively where not normative. In a "he said/she said" story told in dialogue, reported speech is the encoding norm and often important information in these stories will be encoded in nonreported form.

The use of evaluation must be highly monitored and, it is not too far-fetched to say, orchestrated by the teller. The degree of salience accorded any proposition by use of any evaluative device or combination of devices depends on the power of the device or set of devices at that specific moment in the telling. If a device has been heavily used earlier, for example, it is no longer so "surprising" or arresting—a change in effectiveness analogous to the functioning of much "forte" in music. Exactly as forte becomes the "normal" volume and a change to "piano" is strongly perceived, a shift from a heavily used device, such as increased volume or heavy modification, to one which has not been used frequently in that telling so far, will function to bring the material so evaluated into sharper focus.

In addition to monitoring the use of evaluative devices themselves, the narrator must also monitor the relative amount of evaluation accorded the many propositions. In order to assure each proposition the amount of foregrounding it should have, the teller must keep track of how much evaluation each proposition was accorded earlier in the telling. If the narrator used evaluation freely in previous clauses, he must increase the evaluation—either in numbers of evaluators or distinctiveness (or a combination of both)—in marking subsequent propositions he finds more important.

Evaluation of information encoded in one clause by devices realized in other clauses—whether with scope inside the storyworld or beyond it—is called *deictic evaluation* to contrast it with *contential evaluation* in which the evaluating device and evaluated information are within the same clause. Along with comments about the story, there are a number of other commonly used deictic devices including elaboration in later clauses on information presented earlier, generalization from one instance to the general case, flash sequences which give explanatory information, and, often, reported speech. (Except in a story in which someone acquires the power of speech, speaking in and of itself is not usually significant. What is said may be significant or may point beyond to some other aspect of the storyworld indicated by the remark.)   Repetition is the purest deictic device—what is evaluated achieves prominence by the mere fact of repetition.[4]

The same clause may contain evaluative structures functioning both deictically and contentially; some information in the clause itself may be highlighted by one or more devices within the clause, while others point beyond the confines of the clause to evaluate other information elsewhere in the text. Of course, information in that same clause may itself be evaluated by devices elsewhere in the text. One very common occurrence of this multiple evaluative functioning is found in clauses encoding repeated information. While repetition is a deictic evaluator, as has been pointed out, what is repeated may be contentially evaluated as well.

In most storytelling traditions, more than one device is at work in a story text and more than one piece of information is highlighted by a mixture of deictic and contential evaluators. Typically, as Longacre (1976) has pointed out, important information is evaluated by a number of devices acting in concert; devices as well as events cluster at the peak of the action. Particularly arresting evaluators involving a marked degree of narrator participation are common in American oral storytelling to mark the most significant storyworld propositions (Eisner, 1976). External commentary, expressive phonology, and direct appeals to the story recipients collapse the NOW of the storyworld with the RIGHT NOW of the narration and make the reported events and states immediate and part of the ongoing interaction. Often these evaluative devices are encoded in clauses which must be interpreted

---

4 Contentially evaluated propositions are themselves encoded in a distinctive manner within the clause. Most of the linguistic devices discussed earlier can be used for contential evaluation. Again, it must be emphasized that evaluation is not a property of any given linguistic or paralinguistic structure per se. Evaluation functions by departing from the locally established norm of the text: it is a use to which any linguistic structure can be put and is not in itself a property of any structure. Deictic and contential evaluation, similarly, may be used simultaneously by a speaker in constructing a given clause. To be "contentially" or "deictically" evaluative is not a property of specific devices but depends upon the use to which the device is put in the discourse.

as having scope outside the storyworld. The deictic devices point in from beyond the frame of the story—usually from the perspective of the embedding talk in conversational storytelling—at the goings on inside the storyworld. Normally, both some events on the main time line ("story events") and some durative-descriptive information will be heavily evaluated by the teller. Since the most important (i. e. foregrounded) non-event states of affairs in a storyworld are changed significantly by the most highly evaluated events, the "core plot" of a story can be captured by attending carefully to evaluation.

The linguistic structure of the text itself reveals what is most relevant to the teller in a specific telling.[5] Therefore, starting from the information about story structure and the theoretical assumptions about the nature of stories outlined here, it is possible to construct a paraphrase of the telling, an *Adequate Paraphrase*, using only the most heavily evaluated main line story events (*key events*) and the most heavily evaluated durative descriptive information (*crucial contextualizing information* or *CCI*). The Adequate Paraphrase, composed entirely of the elements singled out by the teller for special emphasis, eliminates all incidental propositions. Since a very different story would result if any of the highly evaluated propositions which interact to create the story's problems and resolutions were omitted or overshadowed by other information in a subsequent telling, the Adequte Paraphrase seems to come close to a reasonable representation of the given telling of a story.

2.4 *Constructing an Adequate Paraphrase for a Story*

In order to construct an Adequate Paraphrase, it is necessary to attend very closely to the encoding details of the many clauses which constitute the storytelling text. After a list of main line event and durative-descriptive propositions has been assembled, the weighting accorded each proposition by the evaluative meta-strucutre can be assessed. Eventually an Adequate Paraphrase can be assembled from

5   Unless a teller manipulates these conventions for his own strategic purposes--as happens in mystery stories for example.

the Key Events and Crucial Contextualizing Information. The paraphrase maintains the order which the propositions have in the source text.

The procedure for constructing an Adequate Paraphrase from the text of a story has six main parts:

1. Division of the story into individual clauses or independent utterances

2. Listing Main Line Story Event Clauses and Durative-Descriptive Clauses and Non-Storyworld Clauses

3. Preparing lists of the corresponding propositions

4. Analyzing the functioning of the evaluative meta-structure

5. Roughly calculating the amount of evaluation accorded each storyworld proposition

6. Combining the most heavily evaluated Story Event and Durative-Descriptive Propositions into a stylistically acceptable Adequate Paraphrase which preserves the ordering of clauses.

The first step, which calls for dividing the text of the telling into individual clauses or "independent utterances" sounds both simple to do and relatively unimportant. However, it is neither, but rather is the cornerstone of the entire enterprise and presents its own, not insubstantial, difficulties. Under the rubric "independent utterances" are included minimal responses, such as "yes" and "no," "well," "but," "so", and other discourse particles (whose functioning is a field of study in itself) (Guelich, 1970; Schiffrin, 1982); as well as "you know," "man," and other parentheticals; exclamations; and unfinished phrases which surface in texts in hesitations, repetitions, false starts, and other phenomena. This assorted linguistic material has in common with fully formed main and subordinate clauses and non clausal "complete thoughts" its unitary nature. While in an ideal text the chunking might well be into clauses because clauses may encode full propositions, all of the other structures which occur in a real text must be accommodated as well. Each of these "unitary" words, phrases, or near-sentential utterances may function in the text either to provide the fragmentary propositional information about the storyworld or the speaker's attitude towards his material. Thus, none can be discarded, but each item should be isolated, no less rigorously than the well-formed clauses themselves, so that its functioning in the text can be evaluated.

The text must be chunked in order to divide the various information it encodes into storyworld and non-storyworld *propositions*. Among storyworld propositions, the Main Line Story Events must be separated from the Durative-Descriptive Propositions by examining each clause (or part) individually and making a judgment about its temporal interpretation. Those clauses which are syntactically main clauses, semantically event clauses, and which should be interpreted as events on the main time line of the story, make up the list of Main Line Story Event Clauses. Other storyworld clauses, (including those which are events displaced temporally because they are included in extended explanations or answers to questions), make up the list of Durative-Descriptive Clauses. Non-Storyworld Clauses are placed on a separate list.[6]

The propositions are listed in the order in which they occur in the source text. The temporal ordering of the source text is thus preserved. In the case of reported speech, what was said is represented as subordinate to a matrix verb of saying. If the reported speech is direct discourse, the verb of the matrix clause is an event, while what is said is not. Full references are substituted for anaphoric or deictic expressions and, as far as possible, the clause is normalized into an affirmative statement with the scopes of negatives and other modals relatively clear.

Translating encoding clauses into their propositional form, is therefore, relatively straightforward. As a general rule, the need to

---

6   It is very important to separate out the non-storyworld propositions from storyworld events and states. Proceeding through the text on a clause-by-clause basis is the only way to make sure that the temporal interpretation of each clause is assessed correctly. This assures that the non-storyworld talk is seen to be distinct from storyworld events and states, permitting an analyst to "find the story in all the talk"--a nontrivial problem for those working with conversational stories of the sort we shall be examining in the next chapter.

make many inferences at this point in the procedure is limited. [7]
However, once the lists of propositions have been assembled and
attention is turned to establishing the operation of evaluation in a
given story, it may be necessary to make simple inferences (using
"world knowledge") from the explicitly stated information to the
implied results of actions or other easily made associations. This
permits important textual redundancies to emerge which might
otherwise remain obscure. (It might well turn out that these
redundancies would not be apparent to someone who was not a
competent in a given culture.)

What must always be done, however, in order to build an
Adequate Paraphrase is a careful analysis of the details of encoding
the various Story Event and Durative-Descriptive Propositions.
Changes in encoding norms must be carefully considered and exactly
what information is being highlighted ascertained. Contential
evaluators for each clause are often relatively easy to identify, while
deictic evaluation, since it operates across the text, is often more
difficult. Flashbacks and flashaheads often act as both contential and
deictic evaluators, delaying the action, giving important
contextualizing information, and so forth; along with repeated and
redundant elements, they must be looked at very carefully. As a final
step in analyzing the text for evaluation, the non-storyworld
comments should be examined for deictic reference to material inside
the storyworld.

Once all of this has been done, one can get a rough idea of the
relative amount of prominence accorded each proposition by adding
up the number of evaluators attached to each. In many cases,
evaluators which show a marked degree of narrator involvement
(acting out part of the story, increased gesticulation, screaming, or
"dramatic whispers") should be given more weight than a simple
elaborating detail. Sometimes an apparent evaluative device will,
upon further reflection, appear to have lost most of its force through

---

7 Inferences from the Paraphrase to the cultural presuppositions which
underlie the "plots" is the work of understanding the Adequate Paraphrases
themselves, which will be addressed in detail later on in this study.

overuse. The information so encoded may thus be somewhat less highlighted than at first glance. Often at this point, too, redundancy of information will become increasingly obvious and the evaluative force of *nonelaboration* in a text of otherwise highly modified details may be surprisingly effective.[8]

Once all of this preparatory work has been done, the Adequate Paraphrase can be assembled from the most highly evaluated Story Event and Durative-Descriptive Propositions. These are then combined into a mini-text, small stylistic adjustments can be made, and the Paraphrase is complete. (The exact degree of detail included in the Paraphrase may vary depending on the use to which it is to be put. If only the most highly evaluated propositions are included, it will necessarily be sparser than if all heavily evaluated propositions are included. (See Polanyi [1981] for a discussion of this point.)

2.5 *"The Baddest Girl in the Neighborhood"*

So far, this discussion has been quite theoretical. Now it is time to see exactly what happens when this procedure is tried out on a real story. The story which will be used was collected by Labov and Waletzky in answer to the question, "What was the most important fight that you remember, one that sticks in your mind?" I have named the story "The Baddest Girl in the Neighborhood" in order to identify it easily. The analysis which is presented below, which eventually results in an Adequate Paraphrase of this story, partially overlaps with the analysis done by Labov of the same story and presented in his 1972 paper, "The Transformation of Experience in Narrative Syntax." It is fitting that his analysis be taken up and enlarged in this book because much

---

8   In Richard Hughes' novel, *A High Wind in Jamaica*, for example, the Key Event--a child falling to his death--is encoded in a simple, otherwise unevaluated event clause. Although the results of the death as well as many of the other circumstances in the novel are very elaborately described, the fall is as silent and unnoticed in the text as it was in the story. (Such deceptive negative evaluating is seldom found in everyday storytelling except by tellers skillful in building mysteries and handling suspense and the unexpected. However, we shall encounter some equally sophisticated evaluation and nonevaluation in the stories in the next chapter.)

of the work on story structure presented thus far in this chapter can be traced more or less directly to his insights about the functioning of oral narrative (Labov and Waletzky, 1967; Labov, 1972).

Rather than repeat large portions of "The Baddest Girl in the Neighborhood," the text given below is already divided into clauses. This division does not correspond to the one given by Labov [1972, p. 383] in which nonstoryworld clauses are included in with the clause to which they seem to belong and the text of reported speech is listed together with the reporting clause. The Durative-Descriptive Clauses, which make up the bulk of the story, are marked here with a "D." All storyworld main clauses, are marked with an asterisk to make it easier to identify those clauses which may be Main Line Story Event Clauses.)

"The Baddest Girl in the Neighborhood"

D *	1.	(Well) one of the most important fights I had was with a girl.
	2.	I think
D *	3.	And she was the baddest girl, the baddest girl in the neighborhood
D	4.	If you didn't bring her candy to school
D *	5.	She would punch you in the mouth.
D *	6.	And you had to kiss her
D	7.	when she'd tell you
D *	8.	This girl was only 12 years old
	9.	man
D	*10.	but she was a killer
D	*11.	She didn't take no junk
D	*12.	She whupped all her brothers
	*13.	And I came to school one day
D	*14.	And I didn't have no money
D	*15.	My ma wouldn't give me no money
D	*16.	And I played hookies one day
D	*17.	(She) put something on me
D	*18.	I played hookies
	19.	man
D	*20.	(so) I said
D	21.	you know
D	22.	"I'm not gonna play hookies no more
D	23.	cause I don't wanna get a whuppin"
	*24.	So I go to school

	*25.	and this girl says
D	26.	"Where's the candy?"
	*27.	I said
D	28.	"I don't have it"
	*29.	She says
D	*30.	powww!
	*31.	(so) I says to myself
D	32.	"There's gonna be times
D	33.	my mother won't give me money
D	34.	because (we're) a poor family
D	35.	And I can't take all of this.
	36.	you know
D	37.	everytime she don't give me any money."
	*38.	(So) I say
D	39.	"(Well), I just gotta fight this girl
D	40.	She gonna hafta whup me.
D	41.	I hope she don't whup me."
	*42.	And I hit the girl
D	43.	powww!
	*44.	and I put something on it.
D	45.	I win the fight.[9]

Once the text has been listed, it is not difficult to go through it clause by clause and separate out the non-storyworld clauses which are not numerous, in any case, in this story:

Non-Storyworld Clauses

2.	I think
9.	man
19.	man
21.	you know
36.	you know

---

9   There is some question concerning the classification of Clause 45, which can be used to illustrate the profound problems raised by the State/Event distinction. I am arguing here that *I win the fight* is a state because it expresses the initiating of the state resulting from having had the fight—as does the sentence *The Allies won the war*. It is possible, however, to consider that the narrator won the fight at one discrete moment. Labov apparently did so when he included this clause in his list of "narrative clauses" [equivalent to the Mainline Story Event Clauses in our terminology]. The difficulties make no deeply significant difference to our analysis, in any case, since the clause is unevaluated.

The Story Event Clauses are also relatively simple to identify. However, it is necessary to watch carefully for the flashback interlude in which the narrator tells about his earlier dismal experience with playing hooky. The events in the flashback should not be included in with the Story Event Clauses (given in italics below) since they are not on the main story line.

Story Event Clauses

13.   I came to school one day
24.   So I go to school [=13]
25.   *and this girl says* "Where's the candy"
27.   *I said* "I don't have it."
31.   *So I says to myself* "There's gonna be times my mother won't give me money because (we're) a poor family.
　　　　　　　　And I can't take all of this everytime she
　　　　　　　　don't give me any money."
37.   *So I say.* "Well, I just gotta fight this girl. She gonna hafta whup me. I hope she don't whup me."
42.   And I hit the girl.

The Main Line Story Event Propositions and Durative-Descriptive Propositions are listed below. To avoid confusion, the clause numbers from the original listing of the story have been retained: i. e. "Story Event Proposition 13/24" corresponds to the propositional content of clauses 13 and 24. The matrix event clause of reported speech is italicized.

Mainline Story Event Propositions
13/24. The narrator went to school.
  25. *The Baddest Girl asked* for candy
  27. *The narrator said* he had none.
  29. *The Baddest Girl said* Powww!
  31. *The narrator said to himself* that he could not take all this abuse
      every time his mother did not give him money which she will not
      do because they are a poor family.
  37. *The narrator said (to himself)* that he must fight the Baddest Girl
      and she would have to whup him although he hoped she would not
(be able to?).
42/44. The narrator hit the Baddest Girl (hard).

The Durative-Descriptive Propositions create a somewhat longer list.[10]

Durative-Descriptive Propositions
  1. The narrator had a very important fight with a girl
  2. The girl was the baddest girl in the neighborhood.
  3. The girl made people bring her candy.
  4. The girl punched people in the mouth.
  5. The girl made people kiss her.
  6. The girl would tell people to kiss her.
  8. The girl was only 12 years old
 10. The girl was a killer.
 11. The girl didn't take junk.
 12. The girl whupped all her brothers.
 14. The narrator had no money one day.
 15. The narrator's mother wouldn't give him money.
16/18. The narrator had once played hookies.
 17. The narrator's mother beat him for playing hookies.
 22. *That he would not play hookies any more* was said by the narrator.
 23. *That he did not want to get a whuppin' for playing hookies* was said
by the narrator.
 26. *That she wanted to know where the candy* was asked by the girl.
 27. *That he didn't have any candy* was said by the narrator.
 30. *powww!* was "said" by the girl.
 31. *That there would be times* was said by the narrator to himself.

---

10 The italicized portion of some propositions is the durative-descriptive reported speech governed by Story Events which are not italicized. If the reporting clause is in a flashback and also durative-descriptive, nothing in that proposition is italicized.

33/37. *That his mother would not give him money at all times* was said
        by the narrator to himself.

34. *That they were a poor family* was said by the narrator to himself.

35. *That he could not take all of this* (bullying) was said by the narrator
to himself.

39. *That he would have to fight the girl* was said by the narrator to
     himself.

40. *That she would have to whup him* was said to the narrator to
     himself.

41. *That he hoped that she didn't whup him* was said to the narrator by
himself.

45. The narrator won the fight.

Once the Story Event Propositions and the Durative-Descriptive Propositions have been identified, the next steps require extensive analysis of the evaluation structure of the story text.

Although "The Baddest Girl in the Neighborhood" was elicited in answer to a question ("What was the most important fight that you remember? One that sticks in your mind?"), it contains a great many evaluative devices acting on a number of different storyworld propositions to make clear that the fight described can qualify as an "important" one worth telling about. These range from expressive phonology ("*Powww!*") and sentence and discourse level devices which provide elaboration, specification, and generalization of propositions to external comments on states of affairs in the narrative world ("*you know," "man," "I think*"). Of the many propositions evaluated by at least one evaluative device, many function deictically to evaluate information elsewhere in the text. The most heavily evaluated Durative-Descriptive Propositions ("*The girl was the baddest girl in the neighborhood.*" [Proposition 21]) and ("*That the narrator was poor*" [inferred from combining explicit propositions 14/15/33-37//34]) and ("*That he would no longer be bullied*" [Proposition 35]) and the Key Event ("*The narrator hit the girl*" [Proposition 42/44]) are each evaluated both contentially and deictically. I will assess each of these most important propositions individually.

Since this is quite tedious to follow step by step, this detailed information has been put together in Chart 1, "Evaluation in 'The Baddest Girl in the Neighborhood.'" The chart has six columns. Each clause of the story is analyzed consecutively, each on its own line. The first columns, headed "Clause Number" and "Clause," respectively, are self-explanatory. The third column, "Story Event (E) or Durative Descriptive (D)" indicates whether a storyworld clause is a Main Line Event Clause ("E") or a Durative-Descriptive Clause ("D"). If the clause is not a storyworld clause, it is marked "N. S." for Non-Storyworld. In the fourth and fifth column, the propositional content of the clause is given if it is evaluated at all. If it was left unevaluated in the telling, these columns will both be left blank. The fourth column, "Proposition + Contential Evaluators," lists the proposition and any contential evaluators found within the clause which evaluate it. In the fifth column, "Proposition + Deictic Evaluators," is found the proposition (or abbreviated version of it if it was given in full in column 4) and details of deictic evaluators found elsewhere, which act to evaluate it. The clause in which those deictic evaluators occur is also listed. In the last column, headed "Other Clauses Evaluated by this Clause," the deictic functioning of the clause under consideration is specified together with the clause(s) which it evaluates and with the method of evaluation.[11]

The badness of the girl is explained at great length at the beginning of the story. Ten of the first twelve clauses concern the girl's toughness, one fifth of the total clauses in the whole telling. This girl was *bad*; she would punch people if they did not give her candy. She was a twelve year old *"killer"* (marked word choice) who forced people to kiss her and would beat up her own brothers. This specification is important to emphasize the girls's character and to provide motivation for the narrator to hit her back. She was a girl, and boys in our society do not beat up girls without very good reason if they wish to appear proper persons—let alone emerge as champions of the poor and oppressed.

The narrator's poverty is another highly evaluated state of affairs in the storyworld. The information to infer this proposition is found in

---

11 The chart for "Eating on the New York Thruway" [See Chart 2, pp. 56-58] is considerably simpler than this one because it is based on propositions rather than clauses. It seemed useful to give the full analysis from clauses to Adequate Paraphrase at least once.

several individual propositions and the redundant encoding of the narrator coupled with *"no money"* is a very strong evaluator here. It is explained that **the narrator had no money** (Proposition 14), **why he had no money** (Proposition 15), and **that he might often have no money** (Proposition 31) because **his mother would not give him any** (Propositions 33/37). This last is not because his mother lacks generosity, but because **the mother's family was a poor family** (Proposition 34). The information about the narrator's poverty was evaluated by its encoding in direct thought.

The narrator's impecunious state leads to his decision; he will no longer be bullied. The narrator's analysis of his situation and his generalization from the specific instance to the general case is encoded in direct thought, a shift from the direct speech of previous clauses, and marks a change in narrative perspective from that of the external removed observer to participant in the character's thought processes. His decision to fight back is marked by the presence of the narrator and his appeal to the story recipients with *"you know"* (Clause 36) in addition to the anaphoric statement *"I can't take all of this,"* which chunks the preceding action as one unit and renders an implicit judgment on it: it is intolerable. The result of this analysis, then, is his explicit decision to fight the girl and stand up for his rights, culminating in the Key Event (**hitting the girl**) which is itself evaluated by onomatopoeia and specification of manner in subsequent clauses as well as the contential evaluation of the short non-speech, very decisive, event clause (*"I hit the girl"*). This is the first such clause (and the only such clause, it will turn out) in the story which ends abruptly with the event clause, *"I win the fight"* and gives the result of the action.

A summary of the story which would capture the essence of the most highly evaluated propositions would include the following information:

1. The girl was the baddest girl in the neighborhood.
2. The narrator had no money.
3. The narrator couldn't tolerate being bullied (because he had no money).
4. The narrator hit the girl.

An Adequate Paraphrase of the story could thus be:

The narrator hit "the baddest girl in the neighborhood" because he could not tolerate being bullied for having no money.

This strips the telling of its excitement, of its pathos, of its art, but preserves the information which we would need to ask a question about the story which would show real understanding of what had gone on. On the basis of such a paraphrase, we would be able to tell a "topically coherent" next story by building that next story around *fighting, baddest girls,* or *refusing to be bullied.* A story built around *going to school* or *playing hooky* would need more introductory comment to establish why it was told.

If one were to hear a telling on another occasion which purported to be the "same story" as "The Baddest Girl in the Neighborhood" and the narrator left out the location of the confrontation or the fact that his mother had once beaten him for playing hooky, one would have no serious difficulty in judging the two tellings to be "essentially" the same. The story is not really "about" hooky and we have very little impression of where the fight took place. On the other hand, if the narrator left out the fact that the girl was a bully we would think poorly rather than well of the narrator for fighting the girl. He would emerge as a bully himself, beating up people (assumed to be) weaker than himself. If his poverty were eliminated, we would also lose the point of this story. This is not really about a "fight," per se, nor is it really about "fighting girls." In this telling of these events, the narrator stands up for his rights against a stronger force. It is a story of *courage*. We know which culturally significant inferences to draw from the conjunction of poverty—stronger forces—deciding to fight. For Americans, it is a standard plot but it is not weaker just because it is stereotypic. Rather it is stronger. The presupposed "facts of life" that give this story much of its impact will be explored in Chapter Four following the discussion of conversational story structures in the next chapter.

CHART 1
Evaluation in "The Baddest Girl in the Neighborhood"

Clause Number	Clause	Story Event (E) or Durative Descriptive (D)	Proposition + Contentia Evaluators	Proposition + Deictic Evaluators	Other Clauses Evaluated by this Clause
1.	(Well,) one was with a girl	D		This fight most important (Clause 2)	
2.	I think	N.S.			External comment (Clause 1)
3.	And she was the baddest girl the baddest girl in the neighborhood	D	The girl was the worst girl in the neighborhood. (repetition of superlative)	Girl the worst girl in the neighborhood. Specification (Clauses 4-9; 11-12 by external comment (Clause 10)	
4.	If you didn't bring her candy to school	D			Negative conditional (Clause 3)
5.	She would punch you in the mouth	D			Universal result (Clause 3) detail1
6.	And you had to kiss her	D			Universal imperative (Clause 3) detail2
7.	when she'd tell you	D			Universal conditional (Clause 3)
8.	This girl was only about 12 years old	D	The girl was 12 years old ("only about" - modification)		Characterization (Clause3) detail3
9.	man	N.S.			external exclamation (Clause 8/9 = 3)
10.	but she was a killer	D	The girl was a killer. ("killer" - loaded word)	Girl a young killer: Contrast (Clause 8)	Loaded characterization (Clause 3) detail4
11.	She didn't take no junk	D	The girl did not tolerate what she did not like (?) (negative statement)		Negative characterization (Clause 3) detail5

(continued)

CHART 1 (Continued)

Clause Number	Clause	Story Event (E) or Durative Descriptive (D)	Proposition + Contential Evaluators	Proposition + Deictic Evaluators	Other Clauses Evaluated by this Clause
12.	She whupped all her brothers	D	The girl beat up her brothers (won fights with boys = strong)		Characterization (Clause 3) detail6
13.	And I came to school one day	E			
14.	And I didn't have no money	D	Narrator had no money. (Negative proposition)	Narrator had no money. Repeated specification (Clause 15,33,37)	
15.	My ma wouldn't give me no money	D	Mother gave narrator no money. (Negative proposition)		Specification (Clause 14) detail1
16.	And I played hookies one day	D	Narrator had played hooky. (Repetition)	Narrator had once played hooky. Repetition (Clause 18) external comment (Clause 19)	
17.	She put something on me	D			
18.	I played hookies	D		Narrator had played hooky. External comment (Clause 19)	
19.	man	N.S.			External comment (Clause 18)
20.	(So) I said	D			Direct Discourse (Clause 22)
21.	You know	N.S.			External comment (Clause 22)
22.	"I'm not gonna play hookies no more	D	Narrator will not play hooky (i.e., Narrator will go to school) (Direct discourse)	Narrator will not play hooky. External comment (Clause 21) Specification (Clause 23)	

(continued)

CHART 1 (*Continued*)

Clause Number	Clause	Story Event (E) or Durative Descriptive (D)	Proposition + Contential Evaluators	Proposition + Deictic Evaluators	Other Clauses Evaluated by this Clause
23.	cause I don't wanna get a whuppin'"	D	Narrator does not want to be whipped. (Direct discourse; negative proposition)		Specification (Clause 22) detail
24.	(So) I go to school	E(=13)			
25.	and this girl says	E			Direct discourse (Clause 26)
26.	"Where's the candy?"	D	Girl asks for candy. (Direct discourse)		
27.	I said	E			Direct discourse (Clause 26)
28.	"I don't have it"	D	Narrator has no candy. (Negative proposition. Direct discourse.)		
29.	She says	E			Action encoded as direct discourse (Clause 30)
30.	powww!	D	Narrator hit by baddest girl (Action encoded as direct discourse; onomatopoeia.)		
31.	(So) I says to myself	E			Direct discourse (Clause 32-37)
32.	"There's gonna be times	D			
33.	my mother won't give me money	D	Mother won't give money (=Narrator has no money) (Hypothetical; negative)	Mother won't give money (=Narrator has no money) Specification (Clause 34)	
34.	because (we're) a poor family	D			Specification (Clause 33) Reference (Clause 24-30)

(continued)

CHART 1 (Continued)

Clause Number	Clause	Story Event (E) or Durative Descriptive (D)	Proposition + Cortential Evaluators	Proposition + Deictic Evaluators	Other Clauses Evaluated by this Clause
35.	And I can't take all of this	D	Narrator cannot tolerate being bullied. (Negative proposition)		
36.	you know	N.S.	Presence of narrator.		External comment (Clauses 35-37)
37.	everytime she don't give me any money"	D	Mother doesn't give money (Narrator has no money) (Negative proposition; repetition)		Specification (Clause 35)
38.	(So) I say	E			Reported thought (Clause 39-41)
39.	"Well, I just gotta fight this girl.	D	Narrator must fight the baddest girl. (Necessity)		
40.	She gonna hafta whup me.	D	Baddest girl must beat narrator. (i.e., Narrator will fight baddest girl) (Future necessity)		
41.	I hope she don't whup me.	D	Narrator hopes girl doesn't beat him. (Negative hypothetical)		
42.	And I hit the girl	E	Narrator hit the baddest girl. (Short event sentence. First positive action by narrator. First non "housekeeping", non-reported discourse event.)	Narrator hit the baddest girl. Specification (Clauses 43-44) onomatopoeia (Clause 43)	
43.	powww!	D			Onomatopoeia (Clause 43)
44.	and I put something on it.	E(=42)	Narrator hit the baddest girl. (Repetition of action in clause 42)		Specification (Clause 43)
45.	I win the fight	ED			Result of action in Clause 42

3

American Stories in Conversation

3.0 Introduction

Talk containing conversational stories is composed of a number of clauses only some of which have their reference inside a storyworld. A storytelling may be interrupted by talk which has nothing to do with the telling and may be resumed after the interruption is completed. The resumption itself, in these cases, is signalled by apologies and reinitiation markers ("So," "well," "where were we? Oh, yeah . . . "), none of which are of the storyworld. Even in a telling as seemingly unitary as "The Baddest Girl in the Neighborhood," some clauses may not encode states of affairs in the storyworld but express the teller's involvement with the social interaction in which the story is told. ("You know,", "man," etc.) In this chapter, some of the constraints arising from the social context in which conversational storytelling takes place are considered. It should become clear that norms of proper social interaction generally obtaining in conversation are important forces in determining which storyworld propositions are included or emphasized in a given telling and precisely how they are encoded.

In order to understand these social constraints better, the discussion in the opening sections of this chapter relies heavily on important observations made by ethnomethodological conversational analysts and reported in Sacks (1970-71) and Jefferson (1979). Their aims do not coincide with the goals of the present enterprise. They are primarily interested in stories as "sequenced objects articulating with the context in which they are told" (Jefferson, 1979, p. 219) while this study concentrates on linguistic and cultural aspects of story structure. However, the two enterprises are compatible and even complementary. One must understand the social mechanisms through which individual stories are told in turn-by-turn talk in order to understand the surface structure of conversational stories. Yet, without an understanding of the internal linguistic and semantic structure of those stories, one could not hope to understand the abstract semantic objects realized in that talk.

3.1 Constraints on Conversational Storytelling

Generally speaking, conversations can be characterized as "democratic" because unlike speech events such as sermons, lectures, or interviews, in conversation all participants have equal access to the floor. Turn-taking occurs frequently and in an orderly manner. Considering the opportunities for more than one speaker to be talking at any given time, it is remarkable how seldom overlaps occur, even in a fast and furious discussion. Roughly speaking, clause boundaries mark a point of possible speaker change, and while speakers are under a very strong constraint to make their utterances somehow coherent with what has been going on immediately preceding their talking, this may be taken care of in the very opening parts of the turn, leaving the rest available to be directed as the speaker might wish. (See Sacks, Schegloff, and Jefferson, 1976 for a full discussion of turn-taking in conversation.)

Regular speaker change and the equal right of participants to determine the direction of talk are abandoned when one person decides to tell a story. Because stories are necessarily multi-clause turns (two events and a state clause are minimal), those forced by the telling into the role of story recipients are not free to take a turn after any clause and use the information in that clause as a starting point for their own thoughts (Sacks, 1972). (Think of someone interrupting the narrator of "The Baddest Girl in the Neighborhood" in the middle of his telling to describe how he had once gone to school himself.) Rather, the story recipients must acknowledge that a story has been told by responding to it in some way which indicates acceptance of the fact that it was told and which demonstrates an understanding of what it was about. Should they not do so, they will be assumed to be ignoring the fact of the telling and displaying a degree of contempt for the story and thus for the teller.

Of necessity, the teller focuses attention on himself in telling a story. Not only is he the center of attention while claiming the floor for the duration of the extended turn, but he also makes explicit his judgment of what he believes the recipients would find worthwhile enough to justify relinquishing their rights to the floor. Therefore, by telling a story, the narrator exposes both an understanding of the recipients' interests and the degree of esteem in which he believes he is held. Because socially popular narrators command more attention than less well-regarded individuals (Eisner, 1974), storytellers whose stories "fall flat," suffer a loss of face and bring about an awkward social situation by making obvious their misjudgment of their status.

As Goffman (1967) and Brown and Levinson (1978) have shown, a loss of face for one member of an interaction is potentially threatening to the face of the other participants as well. The shame and embarrassment which would attend a failed storytelling may place the story recipients under an obligation to do something to save the teller's face and thus avoid a painful interlude. This obligation is thus a threat to *their* face, since failing to avoid unpleasantness indicates some degree of social incompetence. This ineptness escalates the teller's loss of face since had he not chosen to tell a story in the first place, the whole problem would not have arisen.

But speakers do take the risk of telling a story. After all, a successful storytelling may enhance the teller's face just as a storytelling failure diminishes it. In order to succeed in telling a conversational story there are a number of constraints which must be satisfied. We have dealt with a number of the more important linguistic and genre-specific constraints earlier:

1. To be a "story" at all, a linguistic text must encode a specific past time narrative description of the goings-on in a unique past time storyworld over a period of time. (A "narrative" description must include event propositions which encode instantaneous occurrences which took place at unique, discrete moments in the history of the storyworld.)

2. The story must have a "point." Cultural initiates must be able to infer meaning from the changes of state in the storyworld brought about by the key events.

3. Linguistically, a story must be structured conventionally. It must include both Main Line Event Clauses and Contextualizing State Clauses. Evaluative meta-information must be present so that story recipients can separate the most salient states and events from the others, thereby limiting the amount of inferencing necessary to find "the point."

In addition, conversational storytellers must take into account the circumstance obtaining in the interaction, which defines the context for the storytelling:

1. The "point" which can be inferred from the story must be relevant to the talk underway and seem to grow naturally out of that talk.

2. The story must be integrated smoothly into the preceding talk.

3. The teller must "recipient design" his story. What is said must be tailored to the specific people who are the story recipients.

When all of these constraints are met, one can begin to judge the story itself—was it "worth" telling, was it really relevant, was it really worth taking up a relatively large chunk of time in the conversation to tell this particular story exactly as it was told, was the "point" which the teller expected to be inferred really illustrated by the goings-on in the storyworld? (In "Fainting on the Subway," discussed at the end of this chapter, there is an example of what may happen in the talk when a story as originally told does not really seem to work precisely as the narrator had expected.)

3.2 *Stories in Conversation Must Be Locally Occasioned and Recipient Designed*

Carefully done storytelling can be an effective and vivid way to explore a matter under discussion in some depth; poorly accomplished, however, telling a story in a conversation can be seen as self-indulgent digression, a blatant attempt to "grab the floor," change the subject, and put oneself forward. Therefore, a competent conversationalist does not begin a story at any random moment, but tries to build a bridge from a point being made in the general state of talk to some states of affairs in the storyworld which can be seen to relate in significant ways to what is being talked about.

Examination of conversational stories reveals that there is almost always some sort of talk preceding a storytelling (called "entrance talk" by Jefferson), which serves as a transition between the story proper and the embedding discussion. Entrance talk often includes a more or less explicit announcement that the teller intends to tell a story. This may be a conventional storytelling gambit such as "Did I ever tell you about the time when? . . ." This is followed by the acceptance of the storytelling intent on the part of the recipients. In the entrance talk, the storyteller has a responsibility to make clear if he believes the story to be topically coherent with what has gone on before or if the storyworld propositions and point of the telling are not really relevant to the preceding talk. In the latter case, the storyteller has a positive obligation to "excuse" the fact that the story might be experienced as off the point. The excuse is often teamed with a justification of the importance of the story to the teller. In American conversational storytelling, complex entrance talk of the form "Oh! Wait a minute! That reminds me. I know it's off the point but I've got to tell you before I forget . . ." assures the recipients that their interests are being taken into account even as the talk is being routed, more or less brutally, into a storyworld.

Propositions which are properly assigned a semantic interpretation in a storyworld (along with the world of the telling, perhaps) mark the actual beginning of the story. Once the story is underway, the pressure to remain relevant to the immediate concerns of the story-recipients lessens. As Sacks (1971) and Jefferson (1979) have made clear, in storytelling, as in talk in general, speakers demonstrate "recipient design" in building their stories. Tellers may choose some aspects of the storyworld rather than others to dwell on in detail or may leave out information troubling to some recipients or problematic in the circumstances of one telling which might well be included another time. If some information must be included because it is central to understanding the point but is somehow distasteful to (some) recipients, the teller may apologize for having to mention it or may implicitly minimize it by hurrying through that part of the story, speaking rapidly, and with reduced volume.

Then, too, the storyteller must take into account the amount of information the story recipients have about various aspects of the story. A story which hinges on the foibles of a particular character will be told differently to someone who is familiar with the person and to someone who knows nothing about him. Failing to give enough explanation could bewilder some recipients who might then not understand the significance of the key events, for example, while giving too much information could insult and exasperate others. (See Schegloff [1971] for an explanation of similar recipient design problems in giving directions.)

The storyteller must make sure that the story recipients have enough information to "understand" the story because the recipients are constrained to exhibit understanding of the story both during the telling and immediately following in the "exit talk" which serves to re-establish the general state of the talk. While story recipients must remain quiet and passive for the most part during the telling—they may not use a turn to start a new topic without "apologizing" for "interrupting," for example—there is a strong expectation that they will show their appreciation of the relevance of the storyworld propositions while the story is being told using nods, minimal responses, laughter, and comments to express interest, sympathy, or surprise. (Requests for clarification and specific questions about the storyworld are also appropriate means to display attention although such comments may be prefaced by apologies for not quite following.) Should the recipients fail to produce sufficient tokens of comprehension, the storyteller may interrupt the forward progress of the story and ask for confirmation that the recipients are, indeed, listening and understanding.

At the end of the story, it is incumbent on the story recipients to demonstrate understanding. After the story proper, there is conventionally exit talk of a couple of turns at least, which revolves around the story. At this time, the story recipients usually show whether the point of the story was taken to be comic or sad, about one event or another, or one circumstance or another. Often a recipient will ask a question about some key aspect of the story or people may laugh and repeat a phrase or two from a humorous story. The teller may also ask the recipients explicitly for a response or even elicit a story on a similar theme from them. By doing this, the teller simultaneously gives an interpretation of his own story and formally turns the floor over to the recipients. Since an absence of exit talk is, itself, a socially salient response indicating embarrassment, confusion, annoyance, lack of understanding, or low esteem for the teller, the teller who initiates the integration of the story into the conversation eliminates the possibility that the story will be followed by noticeable silence.

Failing to understand an appropriate, well structured story is a mark of conversational ineptitude on the part of the story recipients who can be reasonably expected to make obvious inferences and connections. However, because conversational stories are inherently no less ambiguous than literary texts, it is possible for there to be various legitimate interpretations of what the story was really about. In the first place, stories can be thought to be about the main characters or objects involved and they can also plausibly be considered to be "about" the moral which can be inferred from the juxtaposition of the most important propositions. Since stories are complex utterances, a complex of responses may be appropriate. In the exit talk which follows "Eating on the New York Thruway," the first conversational story to be discussed, the first comment following the story itself is made by one of the recipients. Alan's question *"Whadda they do to that?,"* neatly ties the poisoned coke to the incompetent restaurant staff who produced it, by asking for details of how the poisoning had come about. This response demonstrates both understanding of the point of the story and appreciation for the story, since Alan asked for more information about a story he clearly understood. The storytelling should be judged a successful effort.

3.3 *"Eating on the New York Thruway"*

"Eating on the New York Thruway" was told in the course of a dinner conversation in my home. Besides me, there were four other people present: Alan and Alice, a young married couple about to drive East from the Midwest, Carol, the teller of the story, and Bill, a common friend. Everyone spoke at least briefly during the telling. The situation which is described in the story took place during a trip which Carol and I had made from Michigan to New York sometime earlier. The comment which turned the talk to the New York Thruway followed a noticeable silence in the conversation and was topically unrelated to the talk which preceded it.

The analysis of "Eating on the New York Thruway", begins with a look at the entrance talk which led up to the telling of the story. (The numbers to the left of the text are reference numbers assigned to individual clauses. We shall refer to the clauses with these numbers in the following analysis.)

Entrance Talk

1.	Alice:	I'm thinking of packing a lot of food and not eating on the road.There's something so depressing
	Bill:	Don't eat on the New York Thruway
5.	Livia:	Do NOT eat on the New York Thruway
	Carol:	Yeah, no don't it's
10.	Livia:	I think that's a good idea. I mean I'm not a picnicking person, generally.
15.		But God, the New York Thruway
	Alice:	Well, there're those
	Carol:	Even I, (laugh) what a mess
20.	Alice:	Well, it's the standard chain

	Livia:	No, it it's a million times worse
25.	Carol:	Yeah. You wouldn't believe it
	Alice:	I forget
30.	Carol:	I mean I mean Did I ever tell you the story about the
		water? I mean the coke?

When Carol announces that she has a story to tell, (Clause 30-31: *Did I ever tell you the story about the water, I mean the coke?*) she raises the expectation that she will tell a story involving water and coke and that would somehow make clear exactly why Carol (along with Bill and Livia) felt negatively about the food served in the restaurants on the New York Thruway. Because the story follows Carol's statement to Alice that . . . *[She]* . . . *wouldn't believe* . . . *[why the restaurants are a million times worse than the standard chain]* . . ., the recipients were led to expect an "incredible" story, something more dramatic than merely having had indifferent food and poor service. In order to serve as an argument against the New York Thruway restaurants, *the story about the water, I mean the coke* needs to show those particular roadside places in a very bad light. And it does.

The Story

32.	Carol:	I went i . . . I always drink coke, right?
35.	Livia:	Right.
	Carol:	So, Livia is thr . . . walking around with this gallon of spring water and I can't understand why she is walking
40.		around with this gallon of spring water. And she keeps talk . . . She keeps telling me these . . . vague making these vague remarks about the restaurants on the New
		York Thruway and at least we have this spring water
45.		and I don't . . . I don't know what she's talking about.
50.		So we go to this restaurant and I order a coke and I ordered some sort of sandwich.
55.		Now, I don't think you ordered anything.
	Livia:	I didn't order anything.
	Carol:	Right
	Livia:	I sat there making faces.
60.	Carol:	Well, one thing about this restaurant was that every person in it was retarded. (laughter) that's all. The
65.		people who worked there they were one after the other

of the weirdest looking people I've ever (laughter)
70.   either they were retarded or they were let out for the
           day from the mental hospital. I . . . you know
    Livia: They didn't seem to be able to distinguish between
75.   washing the floor and making a hamburger. Both
           things were done in the same way.(laughter)
80.   Carol: So, this coke appears. I was very thirsty. And I went
like   this (demonstrates) straw in took a sip of this coke and I
85.   started in screaming "I've been poisoned" and Livia
           very calmly handed me this spring water. I mean I have
           never in my life tasted anything so bad. (laughter)

Following the procedure for building an Adequate Paraphrase discussed in Chapter II results in these lists of Main Line Story Event, Story Durative-Descriptive, and Non Storyworld Clauses and corresponding lists of Mainline Story Event, Durative-Descriptive, and Non-Storyworld Propositions.

Main Line Story Event Clauses

32.   I went i . .
50.   we go to this restaurant
51.   I order a coke
52.   I ordered some kind of sandwich
79.   this coke appears
81.   I went like this (demonstrates)
82.   [put the] straw in
83.   took a sip of this coke
84.   I started in screaming
86.   and Livia very calmly hands me this spring water

Main Line Story Event Propositions

32/50.   Carol and Livia went to the restaurant on the New York Thruway
52.   Carol ordered a coke
52.   Carol ordered a sandwich
79.   A coke appeared
81-82.   Carol put the straw in the coke
83.   Carol took a sip of the coke
84.   *Carol started to scream* "I've been poisoned"
86.   Livia very calmly handed Carol the spring water.

Durative-Descriptive Clauses

33.   I always drink coke.
37.   Livia is thr. . .

38.   walking around with this gallon of spring water

40.   and she keeps talk

41.   She keeps telling me these

42.   vague

43.   making these vague remarks about the restaurants on the New York Thruway

44.   and at least we have this spring water

45.   and I don't

47.   I don't know

48.   what she's talking about

56.   I didn't order anything

58.   I sat there making faces

60.   One thing about this restaurant was that

61.   every person in it was retarded

64.   the people who worked there

65.   they were

67.   one after the other of the weirdest looking people

68.   I've ever

69.   either they were retarded

70.   or they were let out for the day from the mental hospital

73.   they didn't seem to be able to distinguish between washing the floor and making a hamburger.

74.   Both things were done in the same way.

80.   I was very thirsty

85.   "I've been poisoned."

88.   I have never in my life tasted anything so bad.

Non-Storyworld Clauses

1.   I'm thinking of packing a lot of food and not eating a lot on the road

2.   There's something so depressing

3.   Don't eat on the New York Thruway

4.   Do NOT eat on the New York Thruway

5.   Yeah

6.   No

7.   Don't

8.   It's

9.   I think

10.   that's a good idea

11.   I mean

12.   I'm not a picnicking person generally

13.   But

14.   God

15.   the New York Thruway

16.   Well

17.   There're those
18.   Even I
19.   What a mess
20.   Well
21.   It's the standard chain
22.   No
23.   It
24.   It's a million times worse
25.   Yeah
26.   You wouldn't believe it
27.   I forget
28.   I mean
29.   I mean
30.   Did I ever tell you the story about the water?
31.   I mean the coke?
34.   Right?
35.   Right
46.   you know
53.   Now
54.   I don't think (you ordered anything)
56.   Well
62.   that's all
63.   I mean
66.   I mean
72.   You know
87.   I mean

Non-Storyworld Propositions

1a.   Alice is thinking of packing a lot of food.
1b.   Alice is thinking of not eating a lot on the road (i. e. not eating a lot in roadside restaurants).
2.   Eating in roadside restaurants is depressing.
3.   People should not eat at the restaurants on the New York Thruway.
9/10.   It is a good idea not to eat at the restaurants on the New York Thruway.
12.   Livia does not normally picnic.
15.   The New York Thruway restaurants are too bad to eat in.
17.   There are restaurants on the New York Thruway.
21.   The restaurants on the New York Thruway are a standard chain.
22/24.   The restaurants on the New York Thruway are a million times worse than the standard chain.
26.   Alice would not believe how bad the restaurants on the New York Thruway are.

27.   Alice forgot how bad the restaurant on the New York Thruway
        were.
54.   Carol thinks that Livia did not order anything at the restaurant
ɔn   the Thruway.

Durative-Descriptive Propositions

33.	Carol always drinks coke.
(37.	Livia was thr. . .)
38.	Livia was walking around with a gallon of spring water.
39.	Carol could not understand why Livia is walking around with a gallon of spring water.
37/40-43.	Livia kept making vague remarks to Carol about the restaurants on the New York Thruway.
44.	Livia kept telling Carol (in a vague way) that at least
they	had some spring water.
45/47/48.	Carol did not understand what Livia was talking about.
55/56.	Livia did not order anything.
58.	Livia sat in the restaurant making faces.
60/61/64.	Every person who worked in the restaurant was retarded.
64/65/67/68.	The people who worked in the restaurant were the weirdest looking people Carol had ever seen.
64/69.	The people who worked in the restaurant may have been let out for the day from the mental hospital.
73/76.	The people who worked in the restaurant were unable to distinguish between washing the floor and making a hamburger.
64/75-77.	The people who worked in the restaurant washed the floors and made hamburgers in the same way.
80.	Carol was very thirsty.
85.	*That she had been poisoned* was screamed by Carol
88.	This coke was the worst thing Carol has ever tasted.

As described earlier, in order to put together an Adequate Paraphrase of the telling, the Main Line Story Event Propositions and Durative-Descriptive Propositions are examined individually and those propositions most highly evaluated by the devices operating in the text are singled out.

The analysis of the evaluation is summarized in the chart entitled "Evaluation in 'Eating on the New York Thruway'" which appears on the following page:

CHART 2
Evaluation of Storyworld Propositions in "Eating on the New York Thruway"

Clause(s) Number	Clause Content (Proposition)	Story Event (E) or Durative Descriptive (D)	Contential Evaluators Which Evaluate the Proposition	Deictic Evaluators Which Evaluate the Proposition	Deictic Evaluation of Other Proposition by this Clause
32/50.	Carol and Livia went to a restaurant on the NY Thruway	E			
33.	Carol always drinks coke	D		Appeal for confirmation outside storyworld	
37/40-3.	Livia kept making vague remarks about the restaurants on the NY Thruway	D	Insistence on repetitive nature of comments. modification of remarks	Repetition of proposition.	
38.	Livia was walking around with a gallon of spring water	D		Repetition of proposition in prop. 39.	(Spring water repeated)
39.	Carol could not understand why Livia is walking around with a gallon of spring water.	D	Negative encoding		Repeats prop. 38.
44.	Livia kept telling Carol (in a vague way) that at least they had some spring water	D	Insistence on repeated action.	(Spring water repeated)	
45/7/8.	Carol did not understand what Livia is talking about	D	Negative encoding	Repetition of "not understanding". External comment ("You know" cl. 46)	
51.	Carol ordered a coke	E			
52.	Carol ordered a sandwich	E	(Negative evaluation "some sort" of sandwich)		

(continued)

CHART 2 (*Continued*)

Clause(s) Number	Clause Content (Proposition)	Story Event (E) or Durative Descriptive (D)	Contential Evaluators Which Evaluate the Proposition	Deictic Evaluators Which Evaluate the Proposition	Deictic Evaluation of Other Proposition by this Clause
55/6.	Livia did not order anything	D	Negative encoding. Appeal for confirmation.	Repetition of proposition. Explicit removal from storyworld. "Now" cl. 53. Intrusion of narrator, cl. 54.c	
58.	Livia sat in the restaurant making faces	D	"making faces" - unusual behavior	Intrusion of story participant.	
60-1/64. 69.	Every person who worked in the restaurant was "retarded" or may have been retarded	D	Hyperbole - "every person"	"One thing"points specifically to the "retarded" aspect. Explicit evaluator "That's all" cl. 62. Repetition (3x)	Repetition cl. 64, 69.
64-5/67-8.	The people who worked in the restaurant were the weirdest people Carol had ever seen.	D	people". Superlative. "one after another" Inverted syntax. Exaggeration/speculation.	Hyperbole - "the weirdest 1/64.69/70.Intrusion of narrator cl. 63, 66, 68	Specified further in cl. 60-
69/70.	The people who worked in the restaurant may have been let out for the day from the mental hospital.	D		Intrusion of narrator ("You know" cl. 72) 6c-70 LOGICAL ARGUMENT	

(*continued*)

CHART 2 (Continued)

Clause(s) Number	Clause Content (Proposition)	Story Event (E) or Durative Descriptive (D)	Contential Evaluators Which Evaluate the Proposition	Deictic Evaluators Which Evaluate the Proposition	Deictic Evaluation of Other Proposition by this Clause
73/76.	The people who worked in the restaurant were unable to distinguish between washing the floor and making a hamburger.	D	Mock logical argument. Convoluted syntax.	Intrusion of story participant. Specified cl. 77.	Specification of 60-1/64, 69.
79.	This coke appears	E	First event clause in 30 clauses. Short unattenuated clause. Agentless passive.	Return to storyline, "So" clause 78.	
80.	Carol was very thirsty	D	Comparator.		
81-2.	Carol put the straw in the coke.	E	Acted out. Abbreviated headless clause (cl. 82)	Clause 81. Deictic clause.	
83.	Carol took a sip of the coke.	E	"this" coke. Collapses storyworld and narrating world.	Proposition 84/5 evaluates the result of sipping the coke.	
84.	Carol started to scream "I've been poisoned"	E	Screamed in narration		
85.			Only direct discourse		Points to cause of screaming–prop. 83.
86.	Livia calmly handed Carol the springwater.	E	Adverbially modified.	Conjunction of Carol, Livia, water and coke.	
88.	This coke was the worst thing Carol has ever tasted.	D	Hyperbole. Explicit evaluation. Intrusion of the narrator.		Points to the coke sipped in Prop. 83. Further specification.

The Durative-Descriptive Propositions which are most highly evaluated are:

> 39.   Carol could not understand why Livia is walking around with a gallon of spring water.

> 64-65/67-69.   The people who worked in the restaurant were the "weirdest" people Carol had ever seen (crazy and incompetent).

While the most heavily evaluated Story Event Proposition is:

> 83.   Carol took a sip of the coke

followed by:

> 86.   Livia calmly handed Carol the spring water.

(Since 86 brings together Carol, Livia and the spring water to deal with the result of the 83—the poisoned coke—it should be included in the Paraphrase.)

Thus an Adequate Paraphrase of "Eating on the New York Thruway" could be:

Carol was "poisoned" by sipping a coke prepared by weird incompetent people who worked at the restaurant on the New York Thruway. She was saved by Livia who had brought along (an otherwise mysterious) gallon of spring water.

Alan's comment immediately following the end of the story *Whadda they do to that?* began the exit talk and the absorption of the story into a general state of talk. This question which was delivered in tones of impressed bewilderment manages to encompass all the vital elements of the core of the story: the coke, the incompetence of the staff in the restaurant, and the fact that they must have done something to make a coke so badly. During the remainder of the exit talk, there is a further description of the coke, a re-engagement of the storyworld with a corresponding increase in storyworld propositions, and finally a clear sign from Alice, the other recipient for whom the story was specifically told, that she had gotten the message. The incredible goings-on in the restaurant had apparently jarred her memory about the *horrible plazas or oases* on the highways and she and Alan would make their journey definitely via Ohio, thus making certain they would avoid the New York Thruway entirely.

Exit Talk

	Alan:	Whadda they do to that?
90.	Livia:	(laughing) You see, they also can't distinguish between making a coke and wringing out the mop.
95.	Carol:	Right . . . There is something I mean it was really something
	Alan:	Yeah yeah . . . It's that bad
100.	Livia:	It comes out grey. Bright grey.
	Bill:	And very metallic
	Carol:	No, yeah it is metallic
105.	Alice:	I can't bear . . . you know . . . you're driving and you're trying to make this mileage and you get out of the car and it's one of these horrible what do they call them?
110.		I forget.
	Alan:	Oases?
	Alice:	No. They have some
115.	Alan:	Plazas.
	Alice:	PLAZAS
120.	Livia:	Mmmm hmmm. Oases are on . . . yeah on
	Carol:	On the way to Chicago.
	Alice:	It's horrible. I think we are going to
125.		We may drive through Ohio.

Both the incompetence of the restaurant staff and the exact nature of the poisoned coke are further specified before the storyworld is left definitively. The discussion moves to a more general condemnation of highway restaurants and then back to the topic of Alice and Alan's trip East. Thus, from the exit talk, the following propositions are added to the list of Durative-Descriptive Propositions:

New Durative-Descriptive Propositions

90-94.   The people who work in the restaurant can't distinguish between making a coke and wringing out the mop.

100. The coke comes out grey.
101. The coke is bright grey.
102. The coke is very metallic.

The following clauses and propositions are added to the lists of Non-Storyworld Clauses and Propositions:

New Non-Storyworld Clauses
89. Whadda they do to that
90. You see
94. Right
95. There is something
96. I mean
98. Yeah yeah
103. I can't bear
104. You know
105. You're driving
106. And you're trying to make this mileage
108. and it's one of those horrible
109. What do they call them?
110. I forget
111. Oases
112. No
113. They have some
114. Plazas?
115. PLAZAS
116. mmm hmmm
117. Oases are on the way to Chicago
118. It's horrible
122. I think
123. We are going to
124. we may drive through Ohio

New Non-Storyworld Propositions
100. The coke comes out grey
101. The coke is bright grey.
102. The coke is very metallic.
103-115/121. Alice cannot bear trying to make (good) mileage and getting out of the car at a horrible plaza.
108-110. Alice has forgotten what the horrible plazas are called.
109-112. The horrible plazas are not called oases.
113. The horrible places which are not called oases have another name.

117-120.   The oases are on the way to Chicago.
121-124.   Alice thinks they are going to drive through Ohio.

Although it is possible to amend the Adequate Paraphrase to specify that the coke was grey, that seems hardly necessary. Nothing new is added to the Paraphrase in this exit talk. The recipients understood the point which was made and saw no need to dispute anything which had been said. The point of the story relates clearly back to the talk which was ongoing when the story was told. That talk continued on richer for the story but not re-focused or deflected by it. Having seen how this story functions as a "sequenced object" in the talk and how it is structured linguistically, what remains to be discussed is how this story is demonstrably designed to fit the personal and social situation obtaining at the moment of the telling.

3.4 Recipient Design in "Eating on the New York Thruway"

In order to understand exactly how the telling of "Eating on the New York Thruway" was influenced by the circumstances under which it was told, a number of different types of conditions must be taken into account. Important to consider are the exact nature of the relationships among the people present, their interest in each other, and their understanding of each others' habits and idiosyncrasies. The degree of involvement of the conversationalists in the incident itself is reflected in what is said (and by whom) while the use of humor and hyperbole is influenced by what the teller(s) felt would be acceptable to the others.

Carol's announcement of intention to tell about what had happened to her, while certainly a conventional gambit, was also a real question. Had the intended story recipients agreed that they had heard about the incident involving the water and coke being alluded to, *Did I ever tell you the story about the water, I mean the coke* (Clause 30) might have led to the intended story recipients recapping the story, or Carol herself telling a very abbreviated version of it. She might merely have used the recipients' knowledge as a way of saying "See, that's what happens on the New York Thruway." As it turned out, no one indicated familiarity with the story and so Carol began her telling.

Almost immediately, she appealed to the recipients: (Clause 33-34) *I always drink coke, right?* and managed simultaneously to give Alan, Alice, and Bill some information about her (that she drinks coke), to make explicit to me that she knew my familiarity with her habits (since she appealed to me directly with her *Right?*), and to appear to include the others present in our more intimate circle. Had she used any one of a number of equally possible alternatives, she would have been unable to accomplish these three tasks so neatly. For example, had she left out the information about her coke drinking, her credentials as a cola-conoisseur might well have remained unknown to some of the others. Had she been a cola-innocent, she might well have tasted a perfectly acceptable sample of the beverage and still found it wretched. Therefore, to understand the story, it was important that everyone be aware of her expertise in this particular area.

She might have chosen to state this fact otherwise, of course. She might have stated that she "always drinks coke, as Livia knows." This formulation would have made clear that she and I were closer to one another than to some of the others. This would have run counter to our implicit agreement to act as if we were all equally close friends. Finally, had Carol merely stated that she always drinks coke and left it at that without asking me for confirmation, the closeness of our friendship would have been somewhat denied by placing me on exactly the same footing as the others vis à vis her special likes and dislikes. In fact, we were close friends and knew each other very well.

In addition, and much more central to this particular storytelling, is that I was a co-participant in the events recounted and a character in the story. This story, then, was partially about me and could not but function in some way as a comment on our friendship. To be coherent then, her behavior towards me in the telling had to match the comment she was making about me through the story. Otherwise, the story would function in the conversation as a message which was denied in the interaction as clearly as it was made in the telling.

By appealing to me immediately, Carol drew me into the telling. Having been invited to act as an "expert" and to say something, I was granted more access to the floor during the telling of the story than the others who were more purely "story recipients." In fact, this was most important in the present case because I was as much an expert on the common parts of the source experience as Carol was herself. Moreover, as became clear later on, I was more of an "expert" on the New York Thruway restaurants than Carol was before this misadventure.

All of the vague mumbling and mysterious walking around with the gallon of spring water which dominates the opening sections of the story might well have been played down in another telling. However, there are three circumstances which taken together explain the amount of prominence this mini-mystery is accorded. In the first place, Carol had announced that the story was to be about *the water* before she corrected herself, *I mean, the coke* (clauses 30-31). The subsequent story should make this slip seem reasonable by being *about water*, at least in part. Secondly, since I was present at the telling, that part of the story which most involved me was highlighted more than it might have been had I not been there.

The mystery of the spring water also underscores Carol's own ignorance of the true state of affairs at the Thruway restaurant before she had undergone the specific experience recalled in the story. Like Alice and Alan, she had thought it safe to eat in the restaurant and she had learned from her bad experience why [*Livia was*] *walking around with this gallon of spring water*. In other words, she was mystified and skeptical at the time by warnings of how dire the situation was, exactly as the recipients of her tale are at the moment of telling. What she learned from experience is, of course, what she hopes to impart to her friends. Therefore, Carol, the cokedrinker in the storyworld, is in the same relation to Livia, the water bearer, as Alan and Alice in the conversation bear to Carol, the narrator. The implicit message of the mystery is that they need not feel belittled by not knowing and by needing to be told.

As the story continues, Carol makes explicit that Livia did not order anything. Probably, had I not been there, it would not have been mentioned. Then, too, had she said something about it, she would most probably have merely stated that I did not order. She would not have exited from the storyworld and given her theory about what I had done ([Clauses 53-55] *Now, I don't think you ordered anything.*) Her doing so again reflects my status as co-participant and primary expert on my own behavior. Carol would probably omit Proposition 58, *Livia sat in the restaurant making faces* in another telling of the story, since it is not treated as an "omission" by either teller and Carol's response to it is marked as a return to the main story: *Well . . .* (Clause 59).

It is more difficult to make a strong case exactly why some material was included in this telling, but it seems reasonable to suppose that the remarks about the *weird looking people who were either retarded or let out for the day from a mental hospital* (Clauses 67-70) might well have been omitted altogether or phrased very differently had any of those present a (known) sensitivity either to retardation or mental illness.[1] The use of hyperbole and exaggeration in this section of the story is also very clear. The story-recipients' feedback was important in order to establish that this sort of broad generalization was appreciated and understood.

Certainly the detailed description of the coke itself, as *bright grey* and *metallic* (Clauses 100-102) would be unlikely to turn up in another telling because this information was provided in response to prompting on the part of one of the recipients, Alan, who seemed to have been entirely convinced by the story. Although Alice never responded directly to the story, her very strong objection to the oases or plazas is clearly traceable to the story; before the story her

---

[1] When I have used this story in classes in The Netherlands, students always object to the "overstatement" of the narrator and recipients, in addition to feeling positively offended by the characterization of the restaurant personnel as crazy or mentally deficient. American "audiences," in classes and lectures have never *expressed* such difficulties with the story as told, although, of course many individuals might have reacted negatively and said nothing.

characterization of the roadside restaurants as *the standard chain* was mild and almost positive.

Assembling and examining the lists of storyworld propositions reveals that many of them are related directly to the particular circumstances surrounding this specific telling. The Adequate Paraphrase which was built up is thus the paraphrase of this particular telling. On another occasion, prompted by other topics in a different embedding conversation and intended for recipients different from Alan and Alice, a telling using the incident of the poisoned coke as a basis might well amount to something other than an indictment of incompetence, and a celebration of foresightedness and rescue.

In Chapter Four, concerned with cultural presuppositions, each of the propositions in the Adequate Paraphrase of "Eating on the New York Thruway" will be considered again in order to determine the source of this story's impact. In the remainder of this chapter, however, the relationship between stories and conversation will be examined in greater detail. An example of a *diffuse story*, a *story sequence*, and a *negotiated story* are treated, in turn. Each of the texts under scrutiny are long and complex, involving intricate interactions among multiple speakers. Although "The Robbery," "Kate's Triumph," and "Fainting on the Subway" are very dense and rich in themselves, in order to limit the scope of the analyses somewhat, only those aspects of story structure which differ most from "The Baddest Girl in the Neighborhood" and "Eating on the New York Thruway" will be discussed at any length.

3.5 The Diffuse Story: "The Robbery"

The "diffuse story" is characterized by blocks of story materials interleaved with blocks of conversation in which points of the story are discussed or amplified. The story begins with events which occurred earlier and moves to later events. The story may have several key events (although there is usually at least one) and there may be multiple core plots. What is striking about "The Robbery," which follows, is that it is at least as much a discussion of what did not happen as what did. The two women, Nancy and Susan, recount this story of a robbery at gunpoint, but evaluate most strongly that it is a story about how they might have been hurt.

"The Robbery"

1

Bill: I heard second hand or whatever that you got robbed

Susan: Yeah

Bill: That's distressing. Was it near your house?

Susan: Yeah. We parked down at the hill you know . . . we were walking home. It was late at night and then this strange car pulled up and we thought "oh" It sounded a bit odd . . . and then this guy ran around and around to the back of it and he held his gun and said "Gimme your purse" and I said I didn't have one and I just gave him my wallet fast and he said to Nancy, he thought she was a guy, and "give me your wallet too." She said, "I don't have one" and he started feeling her, you know, and he had an actual gun (unintelligible)

Bill: You were what? You were walking up . . .

Nancy: It was loaded. I mean, I never doubted that it wasn't

Susan: You know, it was real scary cause you know at a whim he could have shot at us

Bill: Right

Susan: and you they were black and we were white and we thought any . . . you know

Nancy: So all I could think is "God is he going to take out everything on us?" It wouldn't have surprised me at all.

Susan: It was really scary

Nancy: Plus I keep saying, I said three or four times, "I don't have a wallet" but he couldn't seem to hear me. I guess because he was excited, you know, and I was getting . . . "Oh, my God is he going to shoot me because I don't have a wallet?"

Livia: (laugh) Oh, God

Nancy: You know, frustration you know . . . So . . . but he was actually thinking about, the one with the gun is not . . . he didn't . . . at first of course I was terrified seeing this person I didn't even know coming at me with a gun like out of a movie or something

Susan: It was really like a movie

2

Nancy: But the guy who was driving was the one that was really frightening

Livia: Uh, huh

Nancy: I mean he sounded like a maniac. I could not, I could
Susan: He was giving orders to the other guy
Nancy: not . . . But she didn't even hear him. You see she picked . . . she
         noticed all these visual things which I didn't notice. I really didn't
         notice
Susan: I didn't hear the guy in the car talking. Right?
Nancy: But he was shouting out things the whole time and I couldn't
         understand a word
Bill: He stayed in the car or whatever and
Susan: Yeah, he was in the driver's seat
Nancy: He was driving the car and and
Nancy: His voice was so filled with hate . . . I never
Susan: It was really something cause see also a lot of cars have trouble on
         that hill and sort of naturally slow down
Nancy: and, you know, I could not understand a word he said because it
         sounded like he had his mouth full of spit or something. I don't
         know, it was something ugly coming out. And that guy could hear
         him cause he was saying things like "Hey, the dude don't have a
         wallet" or something like that, that was me, boy, and then he
         yelled something back you know and he left and he yelled
         something before he left . . . and it was weird. He's the one who
         frightened me and the thing is he'll probably get off because nobody
         could identify him because he was in the car
Livia: Uh, huh
Nancy: Even though when they brought the first witness up—they'd just
         robbed another woman a few minutes earlier
Livia: Uh, huh
Nancy: He was standing by the cops with that guy and when he brought the
         woman up he said "That's the bitch" (laugh) and they got this . . .
         and also he said "I didn't do anything I was only driving the car."
         and I said "Isn't that enough to get him?" "You know, cause," I said.
         "He's the one who really worries me." I guess I said it about twenty
         times.
Susan: The other one was only sixteen, too. He was eighteen
Nancy: And they said "No, he'll get off on technicalities or something
         cause nobody can actually witness him." Of course, we never saw
         him.
Susan: And they both had a record of robberies and stuff like that with
         guns and everything but see, once you turn eighteen everything's
         dismissed. Did you know that?
Bill: You mean all the stuff that you did before
Susan: What?
Bill: All the stuff you did before . . . juvenile and so on
Susan: Yeah

Nancy: Right. Even though even though it was armed robbery—isn't that bizarre? I mean, I would personally rather be robbed by someone, say 25 or 30

Bill: Than 16

Nancy: without a gun

Nancy: Because I think they'd be a little more stable, you know, in general. It may not be true. They might just not . . . They might be even crazier.

Susan: It's crazy when your life is at the mercy of some maniac

3

Nancy: The police were all nice, you know. I'm happy to say

Susan: That was sort of like a movie itself, you know. We ca . . . we called the cops immediately and they came and they had already had the guys and so they took us in his car to where we had to identify them, you see

Livia: Uh, huh

Susan Cause now they take the victims to the place, to them

Livia: Uh, huh

Susan: Instead of the opposite

Bill: How did they, uh

Susan: So they cruised up an down those hills and they found them and

Livia: Uh, huh

Susan: I said "Yes that's him," but see we both thought the car they were driving was different. It was hard to see, you know

Nancy: But she said right away she told me it was a

Susan: Lincoln

Nancy: cream colored Lincoln. I had no idea what it was

Livia: Was it?

Susan: Yes (laugh)

Nancy: And that's how they caught them on the basis of

Susan: But I thought it was an older Lincoln you know because I know the backs of them, sort of

Nancy: And it had a horrible broken muffler sound, you know

Susan: I actually know quite a lot

Bill: Oh

Nancy: Well

Bill: Well, so they were still driving around the neighborhood or something?

Nancy: Yeah. They were just a few blocks away

Susan: The cops had caught them by the time they came to our house which was about ten minutes which was amazing.

Nancy: Well, see, they were going on the basis of that other woman who said she said it was a long white car, white, you know

Susan: Dirty white

Nancy: Right. And they they had already stopped them and then they got our call

Livia: Uh, huh

Nancy: Andso when they came they said "Come identify them. We've caught them." It was ridiculous. It was about five or ten minutes after

Bill: Weird. God.

Nancy: Well, it was just a few blocks from our house

Livia: Did you get your money back?

Nancy: Not yet

Livia: Oh, because it's evidence.

Nancy: And if they're not guilty we don't get it back and you know there're all these things this cop explained to us

Bill: Oh, you mean, you mean, if they, that is, if they, yeah, yeah, you mean if they aren't found guilty then then

Nancy: Right, with all this evidence. I mean, a few minutes later, but it's still . . . so, you know

Susan: You see, I tended to identify him basically on his clothes. He was wearing sort of this, uh, this jersey type . . . what do you call that material? Knit

Nancy: No, I don't think it was jersey, wasn't it just a sweater?

Susan: Yeah. It was a knit but it came long and I said even to her "It's green" and it was green

Nancy: Yes, she did. I said

Susan: she said

Nancy: I said "I don't know. Maybe he was wearing a leather jacket." I had no idea (laughter) I didn't notice anything.

Bill: Well with one auditory person and one visual person you ought to be able to get a pretty good description there

Nancy: Well, my eyes were focused on the gun cause it was about a foot from my head.

Susan: He was holding it like a cop, you know, like that with both his hands.

Bill: Oh Jesus

Livia: Gooood

Nancy: If it ever happens to you, that cop says that's a very common reaction, you know, he said after you've been trained you can take your eyes off the gun cause you know it's there and you don't have to keep staring at it.

Livia: (laugh)

Nancy: And it's true . . . but I didn't . . . you, I was

Bill: Yeah, I wouldn't . . .

Nancy: Well, see, if I

Susan: I'm glad they didn't make one of us or both go with them or something, you know, with the gun. . .

Nancy: Right. Or just shoot us because, you know, for kicks or something.
         That's the the . . . It was the kind of thing that . . . It's terrible to be
         at the mercy of such people, you know
Susan: It makes you want to get a bullet-proof vest or something (laughter)
Susan: Has anything like that ever happened to you? Have you ever had
         your purse snatched?

The story has three main sections narrated more or less in the order one would expect had the story been told as one continuous unit: the robbery, the encounter with the driver, and finally, the incident with the police. (In the text, these sections are marked off from one another by spacing and numbering.) Section 1 details the actual action of being robbed. Discussion is concerned with the gun and the fact that the narrators were not murdered by their assailants though they might have been. Section 2 discusses the driver of the car and is an embedded story, or vignette, which evaluates the driver's behavior and raises the possibility that the robbers might not be prosecuted. Section 3 involves the interaction with the police themselves and Susan's skill in noticing visual details. The storytelling ends with a re-evaluation of the danger of the situation and the fact that Nancy and Susan were not killed.

Below, Section 1, "The Story," is given again, this time divided into numbered clauses. Some clauses have been given special marking: EE if the clause is an "explicit evaluator" (such as clause 4 *That's distressing*, which refers specifically to the fact that the women had been robbed and makes a value judgement about it), * if the clause receives a storyworld interpretation, and D* if the clause is a storyworld clause that is durative or descriptive in content rather than an Event. Events on the main storyline are marked only with an asterisk.

The Story

	1	Bill:	I heard secondhand or whatever
	2		that you got robbed.
	3	Susan:	Yeah.
EE	4	Bill:	That's distressing
	5		What happened?
	6	Susan:	Yeah

D*	7		We were parked down at the hill
	8		you know
D*	9		we were walking home
D*	10		it was late at night
*	11		and then this strange car pulled up
*	12		and we thought
D	13		"Oh"
D*	14		It sounded a bit odd
D*	15		and then this guy ran around and around to the back of the car
D*	16		and he held his gun
*	17		and said
D	18		"Gimme your purse"
*	19		and I said
D	20		I didn't have one
*	21		and I just gave him my wallet fast
*	22		and he said to Nancy
D	23		he thought she was a guy
*	24		"and give me your wallet, too"
*	25		She said
D	26		"I don't have one"
*	27		and he started feeling her
	28		you know
D*	29		and he had an actual gun (unintelligible)
	30	Bill:	You were what?
D*	31		You were walking up
D*	32	Nancy:	It was loaded, too
	33	Susan:	Yeah
D*	34	Nancy:	It was loaded
	35		I mean
D*	36		I never doubted that it wasn't
	37	Susan:	You know
EE	38		It was real scary
	39		cause
	40		you know
D	41		at a whim he could have shot at us
	42	Bill:	Right
	43	Susan:	and you
D*	44		they were black
D*	45		and we were white
D*	46		and we thought
	47		any
	48		you know
	49	Nancy:	So

D*	50		all I could think is
D	51		"God,
D	52		is he going to take out everything on us?"
D*	53		It wouldn't have surprised me at all.
EE	54	Susan:	It was really scary.
	55	Nancy:	Plus
D*	56		I kept saying
D*	57		I said three or four times
D	58		"I don't have a wallet."
D*	59		But he couldn't seem to hear me.
	60		I guess
D	61		because he was excited
	62		you know
D*	63		and I was getting
D	64		"Oh my God,
D	65		is he going to shoot me
D	66		because I don't have a wallet."
	67	Livia:	Oh God (laugh)
	68	Nancy:	You know
	69		frustration
	70		you know
	71		So
D*	72		but he was actually thinking about
D	73		the one with the gun is
	74		not
	75		he didn't
	76		at first
	77		of course
D*	78		I was terrified
D	79		seeing this person
D	80		I didn't even know
D	81		coming at me with a gun like out of a movie
	82		or something
EE	83	Susan:	It was really like a movie.

In "The Robbery," the entrance talk begins with a statement from Bill, the story elicitor: *I heard secondhand or whatever that you got robbed.* (1-2), which acts to put "the robbery" forward as the topic of discussion. Since the previous topic had been exhausted a noticeable moment before (a rather tiresome discussion of whether the guests might smoke in the house), this statement functions to shift the talk away from the temporary unpleasantness, away from the silence and lack of topic to a definite topic—one, in addiction, that focuses on the two tellers since they are the "experts" on this robbery. It happened to them. Susan accepts the topic, *Yeah* (3), which gives Bill the opportunity to respond conventionally to their problems in the storyworld. *That's distressing* (4), and thereby make that distress the business at hand in the actual ongoing interaction. His next question, *What happened?* (5), offers the women the chance to tell their story. Susan accepts this opportunity explicitly with her *Yeah* (6), and then procedes to shift the talk from the conversation into the storyworld with a series of clauses (7, 9-29), all of which are to be interpreted as telling about the states of affairs in the storyworld rather than in the world of the conversation.

The eight mainline event clauses are

11	and then this strange car pulled up
12	*and we thought* ["Oh!"]
17	*and* [the robber] *said* ["Gimme your purse"]
19	*and I said* ["I didn't have one."]
21	and I just gave him my wallet fast
22	*and he said to Nancy* ["and give me your wallet, too"]
25	*She said* ["I don't have one."]
27	and he started feeling her

The mainline event propositions of "The Robbery" are

11	A strange car pulled up.
12	*Nancy and Susan thought, "Oh!"*
17	*A guy holding a gun said, "Gimme your purse."*
19	*Susan said* that she did not have one.
21	Susan gave the robber her wallet fast.
22	*The robber said to Nancy, "And give me your wallet, too."*
25	*Nancy said* that she didn't have one.
27	The robber started to feel Nancy.

Here is a listing of the durative descriptive (state) clauses in "The Robbery" along with the corresponding propositions.

Durative Descriptive Clauses	Durative Descriptive Propositions
7 We were parked down at the hill down	7 Nancy and Susan were parked at the hill
9 We were walking home	31/9 Nancy and Susan were walking home
10 It was late at night	10 It was late at night
13 "Oh!"	13 Nancy and Susan thought "Oh!"
14 It sounded a bit odd	14 The car that pulled up sounded odd
15 And then this guy ran around and around to the back of the car	15 A guy ran around to the back of the car
16 and he held this gun.	29/16 The guy held a gun
18 "Gimme your purse"	18 The guy told Susan to give him her purse
20 I didn't have one	20 Susan said she didn't have one
23 he thought she was a guy	23 The guy thought Nancy was a guy
24 "and give me your wallet, too"	24 The guy told Nancy to give him her wallet, too.
26 "I don't have one"	26 Nancy said that she didn't have one
27 and he started feeling her	
29 and he had an actual gun	29 The gun was a real gun
31 you were walking up	
32 It was loaded, too.	34/32 The gun was loaded
34 It was loaded	
36 I never doubted that it wasn't	36 Nancy never doubted that the gun was loaded
38 It was real scary	38/54 (Being robbed at gunpoint) was real scary
41 at a whim he could have shot at us	41 At a whim the guy could have shot at Susan and Nancy
44 they were black	44 The robbers were black
45 we were white	45 Nancy and Susan were white
46 and we thought	46/50 All Nancy could think was that the robber might take (all the problems of being black) out on Nancy and Susan
47 any	
50 all I could think is	
51 "God,	
52 is he going to take everything out on us?"	
53 It would not have surprised me at all	53 Nancy would not have been surprised if the robber had taken out all of his problems on Nancy and Susan

54	It was real scary	
56	I kept saying	56/57 Nancy kept saying that she did not have a wallet
57	I said three or four times	
58	"I don't have a wallet"	
59	but he couldn't seem to hear me	59 The robber could not hear that Nancy was saying that she did not have a wallet
61	because he was excited	61 The robber was excited
63	and I was getting	63-66 Nancy was getting frightened that she would be shot because she did not have a wallet.
64	"Oh my God,	
65	is he going to shoot me	
66	because I don't have a wallet."	
69	frustration	69 (The robbers might have shot Nancy out of) frustration (because she did not have a wallet)
71	but he was actually thinking about	71-72 The guy with the gun was thinking about (?)
72	the one with the gun is	
73	not	
74	he didn't	
77	I was terrified	77 Nancy was terrified.
78	seeing this person	78 Nancy saw a person she didn't know
79	I didn't even know	
80	coming at me with a gun like out of a movie	80 Nancy saw a person come at her with a gun like out of a movie
81	or something	

At the very end of the story Nancy says, *If it ever happens to you, that cop says* [referring to the policeman who arrested the robbers] *that's a very common reaction , you know, he said after you've been trained you can take your eyes off the gun cause you know it's there and you don't have to keep staring at it.* This is a piece of information, advice really, from inside the storyworld with bearing outside the storyworld. Susan's final remark, *It makes you want to get a bulletproof vest or something*, and Nancy's final comment on the experience, *It's terrible to be at the mercy of such people*, are both general comments from a vantage point outside to the actual goings on in the story, but each has a general point to make that is valid beyond the confines of the story and that can be thought of as the moral of.the story (and the experience) as a whole.

These final remarks of the tellers can be thought of as a coda to the story as a whole (Labov, 1972). They join storyworld time to the ongoing time of the interaction just as the very opening remark by Bill, *I heard secondhand or whatever that you got robbed*, joins the conversational time to the storyworld time of the subordinate clause and functions as an abstract of the coming story.

In order to complete the catalogue of clauses, all that is needed is a listing of nonstoryworld clauses:

1	I heard second hand or whatever	42	Right
		?43	and you
2	that you got robbed	48	you know
3	yeah	49	so
4	That's distressing	55	Plus
5	What happened?	60	I guess
8	you know	62	you know
28	you know	67	Oh God
30	You were what?	68	you know
33	yeah	?70	frustration
35	I mean	71	you know
37	you know	71	So
39	cause	76	of course
40	you know	82	It was really like a movie

An examination of nonstoryworld clauses in this story makes clear that most of them, though outside of the storyworld, function in the storytelling. Some are explicit evaluators (*That's distressing* [4] and *It was really like a movie.* [82]) that quite clearly state the attitude of the speakers towards the events in the storyworld. Others involve questions asked by the story recipients or comments made by them in response to internal story propositions, 30 and 67, for example.

What makes the robbery in our story tellable is clear to all of the participants. First, the victims of the mugging were present in the interaction and were acting as the tellers. Second, the event was recent. Had the attack happened months or years before, the tellers would have had to do more work in telling the story to justify telling it at any given moment. Had Bill said *I heard secondhand or whatever that you got robbed* and referred to a time 10 years ago, the response of the tellers might well have been to ask why he had brought it up at the present moment. Conversational storytellers have to contend with whether their stories are old news in a way that need not bother a literary storyteller, for example (Sacks, 1970-1971).

Once they have agreed to tell their story, however, both Nancy and Susan make use of a number of distinctive encodings to impress the uniqueness of their experience on the recipients. This robbery was not special merely because it happened to them, nor merely because it happened relatively close in time to the time of speaking. It was special for other reasons as well. Let us now look closely at how the state and event propositions making up the story are encoded to see exactly how some of them are highlighted relative to others.

The most highly evaluated aspect of the story concerns the gun the robber was holding. That the robber held a gun was repeated (16 and 26)—repetition is commonly a strongly evaluative device). In addition, the tellers take pains to impress the recipients with the realness of the gun: *He had an actual gun* (29). *It was loaded, too* (32), underscored by Susan's agreement *Yeah* (33), and then repeated by Nancy *It was loaded* (34), with the further insistence from her stance in the conversation, *I mean* (36). This is followed by extensive hypothetical happenings involving the gun: *At a whim he could have shot us* (41), her thoughts that she might be shot *and I was getting 'Oh my God, is he going to shoot me . . . ?'* (64-65), and the identification of the robber as *the one with the gun* (72 and 80). Other highly evaluated aspects concern the reasons why the robber might shoot them, which stem from highly emotional social facts: *They were black and we were white* (44-45), two beautifully constructed contrasting sentences that gave the first definite information about these hitherto very menacing but indistinct figures. This theme of social unrest is amplified subsequently in the reported thought *God, is he going to take out everything on us?* (51-52), where *everything* refers to the difficulties of being a black person in a white society. This is echoed later in the *you know, frustration, you know* (68-70), where an explicit appeal is made to the recipients' ability to understand the implications of what was said. Nancy reports that it would not have surprised her at all had things gone very badly.

When the events of the story are examined, what emerges as surprising is that the events per se are so little evaluated. The robbery itself takes place, as it were, through the speech of the robber who demands Susan's purse (18) and Nancy's wallet (24). The fact that the women were robbed, established in the entrance talk, carries with it the important change of state brought about by the robbery: their loss of money. What was most significant for them, however, was not the event itself but the circumstances of the event—their fear (38, 54, and 77) and the fact that the robbers possessed a gun and were blacks who might reasonably be expected to take out their anger at white society by killing these two women (one of whom they thought was a man) and who could not hear that Nancy did not have a wallet no matter how often she said so.

In the case of "The Robbery," building a paraphrase of the story as told (or at least of that section of the story we have been working with) is not difficult. The most important state propositions can be paraphrased as (1) *the robber had a gun and* (2) *The robbers were black*, while the most important event can be paraphrased as (3) *A man demanded money from Nancy and Susan*. Putting these three together, we end up with a paraphrase that might read: *A black robber with a gun demanded money from Nancy and Susan*.

In this case, however, the point that the two tellers might have been killed, which they had begun to develop in this opening section of the story, is increasingly underscored and built upon. The robbers' gun, too, returns at the very end of the story, as described briefly above, to become the central actor in the story that finally begins to assume the shape of a clash between the two tellers and the gun that might have done them in.

The text is striking in that it is told by two narrators who talk back and forth to one another, amplifying, correcting, disagreeing, and resolving their differences in a continuous exchange. Therefore, the interaction has the "feel" of a conversation. In remarks to an occasional *uh huh* or a short question or request for information (B: *He stayed in the car or whatever and*). Bill also makes some short remarks which are extended signals that he understood what went on. These comments serve similar functions to *uh huh* or *right*; they reassure the speaker that the message is getting through and that it is all right to continue (B: *Oh, you mean, you mean . . . if they, that is, if they . . . yeah . . . yeah . . . You mean if they aren't found guilty then then . . .*).

Let us look at some examples of these storytellers' interaction. Amplification of each other's point pervades this text. For example:

Nancy: Well . . . see . . . they were going on the basis of that other woman
         said she said it was a long white car you know.
Susan: Dirty white

Another example of amplification occurs when Susan reinforces Nancy's point:

Nancy: not . . . But she didn't even hear him. You see she picked . . . She
         noticed all these visual things which I didn't notice. I really didn't
         notice.
Susan: I didn't hear that guy in the car talking, right?

The speakers also ask each other for support on details and reach for accord on what went on:

Susan: You see, I tended to identify him basically on his clothes. He was
         wearing sort of this, uh, this jersey type . . . what do you call that
         material? Knit
Nancy: No, I don't think it was jersey, wasn't it just a sweater?
Susan: Yeah. It was a knit but it came long and I said even to her "It's
         green" and it was green

Only once in the storytelling does a speaker explicitly involve the audience in the storytelling, asking directly if they had known about the situation with juveniles and the law before hearing her explanation:

Susan: And they both had a record of robberies and stuff like that with
         guns and everything but see, once you turn eighteen everything's
         dismissed. Did you know that?
Bill: You mean all the stuff that you did before
Susan: What?
Bill: All the stuff you did before . . . juvenile and so on
Susan: Yeah

However, the story continues to dominate the conversation.
Rather than proceeding into a possible discussion of juvenile law, one
speaker, Nancy, indicates that this problem acts to evaluate their
story:

Nancy: Right. Even though even though it was armed robbery—isn't that
         bizarre? I mean, I would personally rather be robbed by someone,
         say, 25 or 30.

This comment effectively narrows the possible topics of talk back to
the original story by re-entering the storyworld, although
subsequent talk makes it clear that this was a possible point of story
closure:

Bill: Than 16
Nancy: without a gun
Nancy: Because I think they'd be a little more stable, you know, in general.
         It may not be true. They might just not . . . They might be even
         crazier.
Susan: It's crazy when your life is at the mercy of some maniac

Susan's final comment works well for an evaluating remark on the
entire story so far. After the pause, during which no story recipients
indicate any response to the story or attempt to re-enter normal talk,
the story resumes with a general, introductory remark about the
police. This acts as an evaluative abstract for the next part of the
story (Section 3). (See Sacks and Schegloff, 1974 for a discussion of
similar phenomena in conversation.)

Nancy: The police were all nice, you know. I'm happy to say.

The rest of Section 3 consists of a short narrative detailing their actual dealing with the police:

Susan: That was sort of like a movie itself, you know. We . . . we called the cops immediately and they came and they already had the guys and so they took us in his car to where we had to identify them, you see

There follows a short conversational interlude in which the search for the assailants is explained:

Susan   Cause now they take the victims to the place, to them
Livia: Uh, huh
Susan: Instead of the opposite
Bill: How did they, uh
Susan: So they cruised up and down those hills and they found them and
Livia: Uh, huh

This is followed by a relatively weakly evaluated actual identification of the men and a lively discussion of the car:

Susan: I said "Yes that's him," but see we both thought the car they were driving was different. It was hard to see, you know
Nancy: But she said right away she told me it was a
Susan: Lincoln
Nancy: cream colored Lincoln. I had no idea what it was
Livia: Was it?
Susan: Yes (laugh)
Nancy: And that's how they caught them on the basis of
Susan: But I thought it was an older Lincoln you know because I know the backs of them, sort of
Nancy: And it had a horrible broken muffler sound, you know
Susan: I actually know quite a lot
Bill: Oh
Nancy: Well

Interestingly, the overlapped portion of this section is the only one of three overlaps in the story in which Susan and Nancy were truly talking about different topics. Nancy is reaffirming the importance of her auditory knowledge (N: *And it had . . . horrible muffler sound, you know*) while Susan is reaffirming her visual knowledge (S: *I actually know quite a lot*) which refers to and generalizes her earlier claims to specialized information about the backs of Lincolns. This knowledge of cars and color identification of them, leads to a discussion of how the cops knew who the assailants were—they had been identified previously. Discussion culminates in a re-entry into the story, and a re-evaluation of the cops already having the guys from the earlier narrative segment:

Nancy: And so when they came they said "Come identify them. We've caught them." It was ridiculous. It was about five or ten minutes after.

The identification becomes increasingly more important as the conversation unfolds. Both Nancy and Susan concentrate on their own roles in the identification process:

Susan: You see, I tended to identify him basically on his clothes. He was wearing sort of this, uh, this jersey type . . . what do you call that material? Knit
Nancy: No, I don't think it was jersey, wasn't it just a sweater?
Susan: Yeah. It was a knit but it came long and I said even to her "It's green" and it was green
Nancy: Yes, she did. I said
Susan: she said
Nancy: I said "I don't know. Maybe he was wearing a leather jacket." I had no idea (laughter) I didn't notice anything.

Because Livia had asked a question somewhat earlier (L: *Did you get your money back?*), Susan and Nancy must interrupt their exposition of the story and act as proper conversational participants, answering the request for clarification. Nancy, who had been dwelling on the proximity of the assailants to their house before the question (N: *Well, it was just a few blocks from our house*), returns to that point after the question has been dealt with and both interlocutors satisfied with the answer (signalled by L's *Oh, because it's evidence*) and comment:

Bill: Oh, you mean, you mean, if they, that is, if they, yeah, yeah . . . you mean if they aren't found guilty then then

Nancy: Right, with all this evidence, I mean, a few minutes later, but it's
         still . . . so, you know

Nancy's comment (N: *Right with all this evidence*), adds no new
information about the evidence or the judicial process, and then re-
introduces the subject of the amount of time which had passed
between the police being called and the thieves being arrested.

Bill's response to these remarks about the differences in abilities
between Susan and Nancy accepts both of them and leads into the
final wrap-up of the story:

Bill: Well with one auditory person and one visual person you ought to be
         able to get a pretty good description there

Nancy denies her lack of visual acuity (which she had worked
rather hard to build up) and explains that she could not see because:

Nancy: Well, my eyes were focused on the gun cause it was about a foot from
         my head

This comment begins a conversation which returns the focus of
attention to the gun, already heavily evaluated in the story's
beginning:

Susan: He was holding it like a cop, you know, like that with both his
         hands.
Bill: Oh Jesus
Livia: Goooood
Nancy: If it ever happens to you, that cop says that's a very common
         reaction, you know, he said after you've been trained you can take
         your eyes off the gun cause you know it's there and you don't have to
         keep staring at it.
Livia: (laugh)
Nancy: And it's true . . . but I didn't . . . you, I was
Bill: Yeah, I wouldn't . . .
Nancy: Well, see, if I

The story ends with a re-evaluation of the entire story in an
extended coda detailing once again what did not occur:

Susan: I'm glad they didn't make one of us or both go with them or
        something, you know, with the gun. . .
Nancy: Right. Or just shoot us because, you know, for kicks or something.
        That's the the . . . It was the kind of thing that . . . It's terrible to be
        at the mercy of such people, you know

This is followed by a short epigrammatic comment and then Susan
turns to the patient recipients and asks them to tell their own
stories:

Susan: It makes you want to get a bullet proof vest or something (laughter)
Susan: Has anything like that ever happened to you? Have you ever had
        your purse snatched?

One particularly important feature of the diffuse story is that
the evaluation of crucial material is accomplished largely through
the turntaking system of the conversation. In the other stories
discussed so far, evaluation is accomplished mainly through lexical
and sentence level devices with some additional discourse devices
such as delaying the course of the action. Much evaluation in diffuse
stories is carried out by the storytellers who act as conversational
partners, taking up various themes in the story as topics of
conversation. Thus while the actual narration of the Main Line
Story Events in this telling was a somewhat bald presentation of
what happened, in the discussion which followed in Section 3, both
the identification of the assailants first mentioned as an event
(*Susan said, "Yes that's him."*) and the car which the assailants
were driving were evaluated by extensive conversational exchange.

The diffuse story provides a strategy for telling a very long story
with significant emotional impact but few events. The tellers engage
in pseudo-conversation through which all of the short, purely
narrative sections are expanded and thoroughly contextualized and
explored. This medium offers opportunity and a flexibility for
eliciting and being responsive to the reactions of the recipients. Since
the storytellers are quite actively conversing as well as storytelling,
they are relieved of the responsibility for keeping the action going.
In addition they need not determine exactly which potentially

interesting material ought to be conventionally structured and evaluated at the expense of other material. (See 4.6 below for discussion of cultural presuppositions in this story based on an Adequate Paraphrase of the most highly evaluated propositions.)

3.6 The Story Sequence: "Kate's Triumph"

The "story sequence," "Kate's Triumph," discussed below differs from "The Robbery" in three important respects. First, there is more than one story told, and the stories are told as more or less self-contained units, some of which are embedded within others. Second, there is one primary narrator for each story, although more than one storyteller is involved in telling stories at various points in the sequence. The secondary storytellers, who were also involved in the circumstances being discussed and knew enough to have told the same—or similar—story, act more or less as story recipients while the story is being told. Though the primary storyteller is prompted by secondary storytellers, there is no real competition for the floor and the talking remains clearly "storytelling" and not a pseudo-conversation. Third, the evaluation in the stories which makes up the sequences is, for the most part, internal to the storyworld clauses.

"Kate's Triumph" is an example of a story sequence: a long story telling interaction which is difficult to break down absolutely into its constituent parts. The storyworld propositions may arguably be divided into a group of stories interacting either as a simple chain of one story after another; as a hierarchically embedding structure of major stories which embed minor ones within them as vignettes; or as one very large story, hierarchically embedding several major stories which appear independent as they are being told but which link up into one grand unit at the end of the sequence.

"The Ordeal"

Tom: Right. We'd all gone through this ordeal with the stitching and the unstitching and the bleeding and uh . . . you know Kate having . . . essentially . . . what could have been considered surgery done without anything but a local anaesthetic. (B: hm) . . . uh . . . which meant that she was awake and crying out whenever something hurt especially all the pressure (L: mmm) and uh . . . that was not so bad for Kennedy but this Meyers guy, the bowel man (laughter) was really freaked out by it. He's coming up into obstetrics (K: Kennedy was upset, too) delivery room "What's going on here? What are you doing? (laughter)

Livia: Oh, no Kate. "What baby?"

Tom: "What is this?" Well, you know we went through two hours of that . . . and then . . . you know . . . Kate was all ready to see the . . . to see Adam you know she was all pale (laughter) and in need of blood and she's asking a million questions (laughter) UH . . . let's see . . . "Will I be able to get a private room?" (K: laugh) "Can I have the baby in the room tomorrow?" (laughter) "Is it all right even if I'm on the I-V?" Uh "If I can't eat, when can I drink?" "When you say I can't have many liquids how much liquids can I have?" (laughter) "Will I be able to start nursing tomorrow?" and just on and on and on you know she . . . you know you know they're . . . meanwhile they're attaching the I-V putting the water in you know and (laughter) and uh . . . and Kennedy was answering all these questions being very maternal (laughter) and uh . . . finally she said to Kate "Do you have any questions?" (loud general laughter) (very soft distinctive voice) and I guess then Kate asked her "Well, you know, well, what really happened? you know . . . and . . . uh . . . and she said . . . "I'll give it to you straight" uh . . . "You didn't have an enema and there was shit in your ass" (laughter) "and when the baby came out it tore your ass" (laughter)

Tom: "Are you happy now? Are you satisfied?" (laughter)

Kate: "And the doctor's afraid you're going to get infected."

Tom: Oh . . . yeah . . . he's afraid there's going to be an infection and that's why you can't eat and we don't want you to shit for a few days . . . and . . . uh . . . Kate is lying back there with her lips absolutely white . . . her arms are . . . you know . . . she's half dead and she points up and she said to Kennedy (Kate: laugh) "That's what I like about you" (laughter) "You tell everything straight." (general laughter)

Kate: Tom, too. It was great

Tom: Yeah . . . you were terrific

"Interlude"

Kate: My father came to see me . . . I don't know Adam was it was the second day after Adam was born or something . . . and he's riding in the elevator and saying to us . . . and people talking about Brown Brown (laughter) "What is this?" (laugh)

"The   Walk"

Tom: You know . . . you know . . . they moved Kate from a semi-private to
        a private room after . . . after she had slept that night . . . and uh . .
        . the semi-private was in one end of the w . . . way over in on one end
        of the hospital and the private was way over on the other . . . and . .
        . uh . . . she was terrified that sitting on the stitches would hurt . . .
        so she walked . . . you know from one end to the other (laughter) this
        became a story (K: laugh). I mean . . . then nurse's aides would come
        in and . . . they would say "she walked with her I-V all the way
        from one end of this hospital" (laughter)
Bill: dragging the I-V behind her
Kate: Well, they didn't know that basically I was terrified. I mean this
        friend of mine had talked to me about . . . uh . . . cousins of hers that
        wouldn't sit down for two weeks after they had the baby I said
        (alteration of voice as if mimicking speech) "Oh God, that must
        hurt like hell" (sotto voice). I wasn't going to do it. Here I'd been
        through labor which . . . you . . um . . . is an inCREDible expenditure
        of energy. You know . . . and after this I'm hooked up to this I-V . . .
        and . . . it was blazing hot and I was
        sweating . . . and I was (laugh) starving
Tom: You were dehydrated

"Hospital   Hierarchy"

Kate: I was dehydrated . . . and . . . uh . . . there's this descending
        hierarchy in the hospital . . . um . . . you know there's your doctor . . .
        and then there are the residents who check you when your doctor's
        not around.
Tom: FIRST there's the surgeon (K: Mm, right, yeah) Meyers was the
        surgeon
Kate: Oh yeah, right Kennedy really deferred to Meyers which was a
        very interesting thing to see. Then there are the delivery room
        nurses that are really terrific . . . then there are the nursery nurses
        who seem to like holding babies . . . (laughter) then there are
        nurses' aides . . .
        (T: right) . . . who come into your room and they don't know
        anything . . . it's like when I first checked into the hospital, there
        was a nurses'
        aide . . . it was her first day on duty and you know I wasn't really in
        labor . . . and . . . um . . . you know . . . I walk into this hospital room
        and "I'm new here and I don't know what I'm supposed to do."
        (laughter) and you know basically they were all like that and . . . I
        mean . . . you know.

Tom: They go around and they take temperatures and strip the beds (yeah)

Kate: I mean . . . they couldn't give you an aspiring. It's like you could tell them you want an aspiring and someone higher up will bring you an aspirin (mm) . . . it's that sort of thing . . . Um . . . and then the lowest of the low . . . are the cafeteria PEOple . . . (T: right) and they're incredibly young and dumb and so on . . . that first morning or the second morning they brought me a breakfast and I was hysterical because here was this smell of food (L: Oh, God) and I went out of my mind and I just screamed I said "Take that out! That's not for me!" You know and basically I just wanted to eat it (laugh) and disobey . . . you know but . . . they said "It has your name on it. It's yours." And I shook this I-V and I said "I'm on an I-V, I can't eat. Take it out of here!" (laughter) at which point the bowel man appears (laughter) magically and he said "I see your lungs are all right!" (long period of general laughter)

We will work sequentially through the text, beginning with "The Ordeal" and working through until the end concentrating on information about story sequences in conversations not covered previously. In this discussion the third story, "Hospital Hierarchy," will receive the bulk of attention much as Section 3 did in the analysis of "The Robbery."

"Hospital Hierarchy" ties the entire sequence together into one super-story. Each seemingly independent story acquires the status of a sub-unit of the super-story and works in concert with other sub-units to create a coherent story-structure.

In his monologue Tom describes Kate's difficulty during the delivery up to the doctor's final answer to Kate's question. At this point Kate breaks in, evaluates the doctor's attitude in a pseudo-quote and then continues with an actual piece of direct discourse. Tom continues the story which ends with Kate's remark to the doctor. This remark re-evaluates the doctor's comment and clarifies that the evaluated material is not the scatological information, but rather the straightforward presentation of it.

Tom: and uh . . . finally she said to Kate "Do you have any questions?" (loud general laughter) (very soft distinctive voice) and I guess then Kate asked her "Well, you know, well, what really happened? you know . . . and . . . uh . . . and she said . . . "I'll give it to you straight"

uh . . . "You didn't have an enema and there was shit in your ass"
(laughter) "and when the baby came out it tore your ass" (laughter)

Tom: "Are you happy now? Are you satisfied?" (laughter)

Kate: "And the doctor's afraid you're going to get infected."

Tom: Oh . . . yeah . . . he's afraid there's going to be an infection and
that's why you can't eat and we don't want you to shit for a few
days . . . and . . . uh . . . Kate is lying back there with her lips
absolutely white . . . her arms are . . . you know . . . she's half dead
and she points up and she said to Kennedy (Kate: laugh) "That's
what I like about you" (laughter) "You tell everything straight."
(general laughter)

Following the general laughter which greeted the story and
signalled its acceptance by the other people present, Kate
ambiguously validates both the entire childbirth experience and
the doctor's treatment of her:

Kate: Tom, too. It was great.

Tom responds to Kate by pointing to Kate's behavior during the
birth process and once again emphasizes that the story is about
Kate's spirit and endurance:

Tom: Yeah . . . you were terrific

Kate then begins what appears to be a story, but which actually
is an evaluative remark about her entire hospital stay. Not only
Tom and Kate thought that their experience was unique and
therefore storyworthy but the entire hospital was talking about it:

Kate: My father came to see me . . . I don't know Adam was it was the
second day after Adam was born or something . . . and he's riding in
the elevator and saying to us . . . and people talking about Brown
Brown (laughter) "What is this?" (laugh)

Tom then begins the second major story, "The Walk," which in his
version has the same point as his explicit external evaluation of
"The Ordeal": Kate was terrific. Kate, however, takes over the
story after Tom had completed narrating the events and presents a
short vignette explaining why she walked. This explanation re-

establishes her human fallibility and creates a new type of solidarity with the story recipients who otherwise might have felt themselves permanently one-upped by such a display of courage. Acting as an intermediary between teller and audience is one of the functions of a secondary storyteller who can spur the primary teller on to tell a more interesting story, or re-evaluate material in the story to make it more credible or otherwise acceptable to the audience (Sacks, 1971).

Kate then tells the third story, "Hospital Hierarchy," which is structured in an exceedingly interesting manner. The story is not only temporally structured as most American stories are, but also mirrors the descending hospital hierarchy which it describes. At each step down the hierarchy there is commentary on the type of person who is at that level. The doctors and surgeon are mentioned only as being on the top. The delivery room nurses, one step down the ladder, are given a bit more color (K: . . . *then there are the delivery room nurses that are really terrific.*) The nursery nurses, another step down, are simply dismissed (K: [*they*] . . . *seem to like holding babies*) while the nurses' aides merit an entire vignette detailing their incompetence and general uselessness. The action of the story involves an interaction between Kate and the cafeteria workers:

Kate: Um . . . and then the lowest of the low . . . are the cafeteria PEOple . . . (T: right) and they're incredibly young and dumb and so on . . . that first morning or the second morning they brought me a breakfast and I was hysterical because here was this smell of food (L: Oh, God) and I went out of my mind and I just screamed I said "Take that out! That's not for me!" You know and basically I just wanted to eat it (laugh) and disobey . . . you know but . . . they said "It has your name on it. It's yours." And I shook this I-V and I said "I'm on an I-V, I can't eat. Take it out of here!" (laughter) at which point the bowel man appears (laughter) magically and he said "I see your lungs are all right!" (long period of general laughter)

The unexpected appearance of the bowel man, from the top of the hierarchy and from the very first story, into an interchange between Kate and the cafeteria worker from the bottom of the hierarchy creates a magic moment in the storytelling. The hierarchy collapses as both ends of the scale come together. In telling her story, Kate uses the deictic this to describe her I-V and shakes her arm as if shaking the I-V and shouts in the conversational setting as she shouts in the story. This acts to collapse the time frames of the storytelling and the story into one powerful moment which simultaneously evaluates her strength as a person (one main point of the story) and the intensity of the experience (the other point). The doctor's final remark which finishes the story (K: . . . *he said "I see your lungs are all right"*) adds even more to the collapse of all time frames since two of Kate's more immediately striking attributes are her strong speaking voice and exceptional verbal forthrightness. These attributes were present in the storytelling context, in the third story, and also in the first story which could also have been summed up by someone saying *"I see your lungs are all right."*

This collapse of all time frames and important characterological material into one instant in the third story leads to the argument that one could consider the whole of "Kate's Triumph" to be one story which culminates in the key evaluative remark in the core plot of the third story. However, each of the sub-stories composing the super-story is distinct. Each story unit could easily stand alone and indeed appears to do so as we proceed through the text. (The vignettes do not really stand alone as told, although they contain enough information from which to fashion a story.) The short "Interlude" in which Kate describes her father riding up in the elevator and overhearing everyone talking about her is not really a story, because it has no point beyond its evaluative effect on the other stories. This question of what can be taken to be the point of a story and what kinds of material provide enough support for the claim being made for the story by the speaker's evaluation of it is discussed below in connection with negotiating the point of a story.

3.7 The Negotiated Story: "Fainting on the Subway"

Story texts, as we have seen, are often complex and bewildering. We may well have a difficult time understanding the boundaries between the conversation and the story, and, in the case of the diffuse story, we may be quite justified in questioning the meaningfulness of such a division into story and nonstory. In interactively constructed discourse, such as conversational storytelling, "meaning" is not an absolute characteristic of texts. In the course of an interaction, proposals for what is going on in the telling may be brought forward by the teller through internal evaluation and explicit commentary and may be disputed by the conversational recipients who may offer their own interpretations of what the telling should be taken to be about. In the remainder of this chapter, we will examine one story, "Fainting on the Subway," in some detail, in order to illustrate the notion of "negotiating the point" of a story.

"Fainting on the Subway" was elicited by Deborah Tannen from one of three or four women in answer to the question "Have you ever had any interesting experiences on the subway?" (It appears here with her permission.) The narration of events and descriptive information was interrupted several times by everyone present (including the storyteller) who asked questions, made comments, laughed, and made sounds of assent. The storyteller resumed speaking after each interruption and backtracked in their story, offering new information about the time of the incident, and made general comments dealing with those conditions of her life and in the world which she considered her story to be illustrating. Most people listening to or reading this text for the first time find it highly complex and confusing, with a great deal of extraneous material getting in the way of the story. Upon closer examination, it appears that what is going on can be best viewed as "negotiation" between narrator and audience about what is to be taken as the point of the story.

In order to characterize this text as a "negotiation," a model of what a "negotiation" involves is needed. Let us take the simplest possible model, and assume that there must be negotiators, something on the table to be negotiated about, proposals and counterproposals put forward, backed by supporting evidence, argumentation, or other manifestations of power, and finally, either resolution of the issue on the table or an impasse reached. All of these features are present in some form in the "Fainting on the Subway" text: the negotiators are the speaker and her audience, specifically those who question and challenge her. Her reputation in the group as both a good story teller and competent member of society is at stake along with the point of the story she has told. The resolution comes with the speaker re-evaluating her story as illustrating a point all agree is both storyworthy and properly backed up by the story materials; then the discussion moves on to a new story.

"Fainting on the Subway"

A: I just had . . . two p . . . particular incidents that I remember . . . and one-uh- . . . [I] neither one of them really had . . . any kinds of endings or anything, that you know resolution, they just happened . . . um . . . ONE of them was-uh . . . back in . . . what 66? . . . . 67 . . . when [?] I (?) FAINted on the subway . . . It was very um . . . uh . . . FRIGHTening experience . . . I had DON'T even remember FAINTing before in my life let alone on the subway . . . And uh- . . . it was a h . . . very hot . . . August day . . . and I was going into the city . . . from Queens? . . . A-nd . . . I was standing . . . in a very crowded car . . . And I remember standing . . . I was standing up . . . and I remember holding on to the . . . center pole . . . and . . . I remember (chuckle) saying to myself . . . there is a person over there that's falling to the ground . . . And that person was me . . . And I couldn't . . .

B: Oh, wow

A: . . . put together the fact . . . that . . . there was someone fainting and that someone was . . . And I just fell down . . . (clears throat) then all of a sudden there was a lot of space, and . . . people . . . helped me up, and . . . someone sat me down . . . A-nd then-uh-. . .

B: It wasn't rush hour

A: Yes it was . . .

B: Yeah?

A: That's . . . partly why I fainted . . .

B: Mm

A: Uh . . . I was under . . . tremendous . . . emotional pressure at the time . . .

B: Mm

A: and personal . . . pressure . . . and . . . the crush . . . of the BODIES . . . and the no [?] AIR in the CAR . . . and everything just kind of combined . . .

B: Mm

A: A-nd um- . . . it was incredibly HOT, . . . a-nd uh- . . . we waited . . .
      until the next stop, (low pitch and amplitude ————) which was
      just a few minutes away . . . and then . . someone took me off . . . the
      car, . . . and (sighs) he got a policeman . . . and . . . he came over . . .
      and asked what was wrong, and he asked me just two questions. "Are
      you pregnant?" . . . To which I said no. I mean they . . . like he was
      told that I had fainted . . .

B: (chuckle)

A: A-nd uh, . . . uh he said . . . in a very embarrassed kind of way do you
      have your period now . . .

B: (laugh)

A: And I said no . . . A-nd then he said OK and he sat me down, and
      they got an ambulance . . . and the ambulance ca-me, and took me to .
      . . a nearby hospital . . . A-nd u-m . . . I just stayed in the . . .
      emergency room . . .
      for . . . I guess an hour . . . It was it was heat prostration . . . A lot of it
      . . .

B: Mm

A: Having eaten . . . having . . . having not had . . . not . . . EATen . . . for
      several DA-YS . . .

B: uh

A: and . . . I was job hun [?] it was just . . . a whole mess . . . BUT . . . u-m .
      . . AFTER THAT , . . . I could not . . . ride . . . on the subway . . . And to
      this day I have trouble . . . riding on the subway . . . If I'm with
      someone I feel
      OK . . . . If I'm alone, . . . IN rush hour . . . I c . . . I . . . c-an't. If . . . I'm
      very very scared of . . . fainting again . . . Um . . . I don't know if
      you've ever

B: Um

A: experienced . . .

B: I haven't

A: . . . There is NO experience in the WORLD . . . like experiencing . . .
      rush hour . . . in the subway . . . Uh- . . .

B: Oh, rush hour. Not fainting

A: Yeah. The closest thing I can compare it to, and I never experienced
      THAT . . . and it's probably a FRACtion of what THAT experience
      was, . . . but I think . . .

B: Mm

A: of the way the Jews . . . were herded

B: Mm

A: into the cattle cars . . . Tsk and that's . . . you know . . . maybe . . .
      maybe part of THAT . . . ties into that . . . kind of . . .

B: Yeah

A: thing . . . And I just panic . . . I mean . . . everything in me . . . freezes
        up, and I can't do it . . .

B: Mm

A: And it's just dehumanizing . . .

B: But people were pretty nice, hm?

A: People . . . are . . . Always nice when there's a crisis like that . . .
        And . . . and the context was right . . . I was WHITE . . . I was a young
        woman
        . . . I was w-ell dressed, I was . . . obviously not . . . a pervert, or a
        deviate, . . . or a criminal . . .

B: (laugh)

A: HAD I BEEN . . . had I been . . . anything OTHER than that . . . I
        could've fallen . . . and they would've stepped OVER me . . . Or
        perhaps ON ME . . .

B: (laugh)

A: I was just saying . . . I . . . yeah, . . . But I was in . . . standing in the
        center of the car, holding onto the center POLE, . . . and I just slid
        down the pole . . . A-nd uh-...it was funny because . . . in my HEAD . .
        . I said . . . my aWAREness was such . . . that . . . that I said to
        myself . . . gee wizz there's a PERson over there, falling DOWN.
        And that person was me.

B: It's weird . . . mm

A: Ok that was . . . that experience

The following list of proposals for what the story told by the
speaker should be taken to be about will be developed at some length
through the rest of this chapter. The reader may find it helpful to
refer to this list as well as to the story itself while proceeding
through the discussion.

Proposals for Meaning

1. Fainting on the Subway is frightening.
    (Proposed by speaker through comments and internal
    evaluation of her story.)

2A.   Personal problems in the past are important.
    (Proposed by speaker in response to B's comment indicating lack
    of proper response to the story.)

2B. Personal problems in the present are even more important.
    (Proposed by speaker at end of narrative portion of story.)

3.   Rush hour is as terrible as living through Nazi concentration
    camp horrors.
    (Proposed by speaker following recital of present-day
    difficulties resulting from the fainting episode.)

4A.   People are nice.
(Proposed by B—citing evidence of how strangers treated
speaker as proof of people being "human" not "dehumanized.")

4B.   People aren't really nice—they are bigots.
(Proposed by speaker, as something that could be a compromise
position. Everyone knows New Yorkers are scarcely human at
best.)

6.   Speaker is an inept subway rider.
(Proposed by C—since speaker fell, perhaps she did not know
how to ride the subway properly.)

7.   Fainting warps perception.
(Initially speaker included this proposal as part of her
description of fainting—but she put little stress on the point. At
the end of the text she re-enters the narrative at the moment of
fainting and evaluates he awareness of herself fainting as the
interesting materials using internal evaluative devices.)

The speaker does not choose to highlight a part of her story
which could have been emphasized. This missing proposal, that
men are convinced that whatever happens to women happens
because of their "biological functioning," will be known as *Men Are
All Like That* and it will be discussed after the others. Discussing an
event which is not evaluated, but might have been, can give some
interesting insight into the process of evaluation and the choices
narrators make about the treatment of their story materials.

3.7.1 Negotiating the Point of a Story

The speaker begins her story with the comment that she remembered
two particular incidents on the subway. She proposed that the point
of her story will be that she fainted while on the subway and that
this was a very frightening experience. Her opening remarks are
highly evaluated:

A: I FAINted on the subway . . . It was very um . . . uh . . FRIGHTening
experience . . . I had DON'T even remember FAINTing before in my
life let alone on the subway .

She uses heightened stress, repetition, and most interestingly, a
negative proposition, i. e. a statement of something which did not

happen to impress upon her audience both the uniqueness of the event in her life and its frightening quality.

The amount of discussion before the act itself, the discussion of the altered awareness, the putting forward of a negative proposition (what she couldn't *put together*) and finally the simply stated event, *I just fell down*, act to spotlight the act of fainting. This is the first event in the narrative structure of the story; it is the first, unqualified remark the speaker has made. Thus it contrasts starkly with the surrounding, rather discursive, contextualizing material. However, nothing particularly frightening happens to her as she is fainting or after she faints.

When B comments *"It wasn't rush hour,"* the speaker knows that she had not really set the scene for her story or justified why this fainting spell had occurred. Realizing that she is losing her audience, she puts forward Proposal 2, *Personal problems*, and suggests that she fainted because she was having difficulties in her life at that time. Although she says that it was rush hour, she goes on to volunteer personal information about the *tremendous emotional pressure* she was under at the time of the incident. There is no reason to believe that this whole issue of *pressure* would have been introduced, at least not at this time, without B's remark. The teller's *And then* which preceded B's question indicates that the speaker was about to go on with the narrative events and not pause for evaluative or descriptive details. By divulging the seemingly extraneous information that she was under pressure, the speaker assures the audience that this is no mere story about a fainting spell, but also sheds light on her emotional life. The idea of personal pressure is evaluated by repetition:

A: I was under . . . tremendous . . . emotional pressure at the time . . . and personal . . . pressure

The use of the intensifier *tremendous* also acts to reinforce the importance of the statement. The speaker goes on to give several details of the conditions in the subway car, and the conditions in her

life which *just sort of combined . . . (into) . . . a whole mess.* Before
continuing with the narrative events, she says:

A: the crush of the bodies . . .and the no . . . AIR in the CAR, . . . and
       everything just kind of combined . . . . a-nd um . . . it was incredibly
       HOT

After finishing with the narrative portion, she comments:

A: Having eaten . . . having . . . having not had . . . not EATen for
       several DAYS . . . and I was job hunting it was just a whole mess.

A great deal or repetition, hesitation, heightened stress, and the
choice of *the crush of the bodies* as an encoding for *crowded*, combine
to give a very vivid impression of exactly what *personal pressure* is
involved.

The speaker demonstrates that this period was a very
storyworthy one, because it differed so widely from the way things
ought to be. She does not stop with detailing her problems in the
past, however, but continues to tell how the effects of this time and
this incident continue on into the present. A story with ramifications
for the present moment is most certainly narratable:

A: And to this day I have trouble . . . riding on the subway. If I'm with
       someone I feel OK . . . If I'm alone . . . IN rush hour, I c . . . I c-an't.
       If . . . I'm very very scared of . . . fainting again.

She uses few evaluative devices in this section, although the
hesitation and self-correction are unusual and evaluatory in the
sense that they almost act out the effects of being afraid and under
the spell of that experience. Her increased stress on the *in* of *in rush
hour* makes certain that no one will misunderstand and assume she
fainted without cause. The double intensifier *very very*, which is
common in many discourses, is only found in this one instance in this
text, lending it increased weight. If past problems are interesting,
present ones are that much more so.

By bringing the effects of this experience into the present, the
speaker is bringing it closer to her audience, insisting that this is not

merely a story about the past, but is a story about the present and an explanation of why she is less than totally competent at carrying out the comings and goings of everyday life.

Unfortunately, the speaker did not stop with demonstrating how this story could account for important aspects of her present life, but insisted that, in fact, this story shows how rush hour in the subway is one of the worst and most unusual experiences in the world.

A: I don't know if you've ever . . . experienced . . .
B: I haven't
A: There is NO experience in the WORLD, . . . like experiencing rush hour . . . in the subway . . . uh . . .
B: Oh, rush hour. Not fainting.

Her own life, past and present, is interesting and storyworthy but since the elicitation question had to do with the *subways* not merely with personal events, she must somehow link her feelings of pressure, heat, and discomfort with some general fact about subways. B's interjection *Oh, rush hour. Not fainting,* seems to be a surprised reaction to the violation of the expectation that the speaker had set up when she followed *I don't know if you've ever experienced* with a discussion of rush hour instead of continuing with the preceding theme—*fear of fainting again.* (B may have been particularly surprised since she knows that the speaker knows B to be a New Yorker who presumably would have been on the subway, under all types of conditions.)

Proposal 3, *Rush hour is as terrible as living through Nazi concentration camp horrors,* is the most highly evaluated proposal, but it is not accepted by the audience:

A: Yeah. The closest thing I can compare it to, and I never experienced THAT . . . and it's probably a FRACtion of what THAT experience was, . . . but I think . . . of the way the Jews . . . were herded into the cattle cars . . . Tsk and that's . . . you know . . . maybe . . . maybe part of THAT . . . ties into that . . . kind of thing . . . And I just panic . . . I mean . . . everything in me . . . freezes up, and I can't do it . . . And it's just dehumanizing

All of the qualification acts to reinforce the comparison Speaker is making. *Tsk, I mean,* and *you know,* which are very common in the speech of many people, are found almost nowhere in this text. The *you know* acts in concert with the unfinished question she asked B and creates an appeal to the audience. The speaker gives the impression that any good person must understand the implications (and thus the truth) of what she is saying by her strong insistence on that, together with her faith that the audience knows the full extent of the evils concealed in the stressed and repeated *that,* the referent of which is clearly the Nazi atrocities, summoned up with the rather formal, almost literary, *the way the Jews were herded into the cattle cars.* The triple *the* acts to impress the certainty of the belief the speaker has in her listeners knowing that the reference is to the Nazis, who epitomize everything that men ought not to be, and to life in the concentration camps, which epitomizes everything life should not be. This is an example of what might be called "evaluation by touchstone"—anything which is compared to the horror of Nazi Germany is highlighted by the strength of the reaction to the concentration camps. Since the rush hour brings to mind the Nazi atrocities, it is of necessity important. *I think of the way the Jews were herded into the cattle cars* is also an example of reported thought. In addition, the expression itself is something of a cliché along with *I just panic and everything in me just freezes up.* Far from diminishing their effect, the very set nature of the phrasing, found seldom in her telling, reinforces the speaker's point. Her final sentence, *It's just as dehumanizing,* continues the animal motif first detected in *herd* and *cattle car,* giving an impression of a more general metaphor of beastliness. *Dehumanizing* itself is an interesting lexical choice, notable for its formal, almost scientific tone.

The essence of Proposal 3 is that during rush hour in the subways people are so deprived of their basic needs of air, space, and individuality that they become like beasts.

B obviously does not accept that the speaker's story demonstrates that people were dehumanized by the conditions in the subway, causing the speaker to faint. On the contrary, she asks the speaker:

B: But people were pretty nice, hm?

She does not indicate that she disagrees with any of the presuppositions of Proposal 3, but merely that she did not believe that the facts recounted by the speaker justified characterizing those who ride on the subways during rush hour as *dehumanized*. The adversative conjunction *but* and the request for an answer indicated by *hm* leave the teller no choice but to debate whether people were indeed nice. Proposal 4, *People are nice*, relies upon the information in the speaker's own story detailing the concern of strangers on the crowded subway:

A: then all of a sudden there was a lot of space and . . . people . . .
          helped me up, and . . . someone set me down . . . . and then . . .
          someone took me off . . . the car, . . . and he got a policeman . . . and
          he came over . . . and asked what was wrong and he asked me just
          two questions . . . and he sat me down, and they got an ambulance, . . .
          and the ambulance came, and took me to . . . a nearby hospital.

All of these are the actions of people acting properly toward a stranger, being *nice*, in a word.
    The speaker's answer to B's proposal 4A is very ingenious. Far from denying that people were *nice* as shown prima facie by her own story, she accepts that they did, in fact, *act* in ways which were *nice*:

A: People . . . are . . . Always nice when there's a crisis like that

but she goes on to deny that they were really nice:

A: And . . . the context was right . . . I was WHITE, . . . I was a young
         woman . . . I was we-ll dressed, I was obviously not a pervert, or a
         deviate... or a criminal . . . HAD I BEEN . . . had I been . . . anything
         OTHER than that . . . I could've fallen . . . and they would've
         stepped OVER me . . . or perhaps ON me.

Since stepping on people who are not white or well dressed, or
even failing to extend help to everyone, is not being *nice*, but is,
instead, being "bigoted," which is quite opposed to "niceness," the
speaker's answer solidly rejects B's proposal. The heightened stress
leaves no question that the strangers were only *nice* because she was
not other than what she was. The repetition of *had I been*, as well as
the graphic description of a purely hypothetical situation in which
she was *OTHER*, join with the large number of details of exactly
what she was (totally acceptable) and what she was not (a despised
member of society) to leave no question that for the speaker her story
could not be taken as an instance of *People being nice*.

The speaker has a counterproposal, however. At the end of her
long description of how *people are not really nice*, she suggests
Proposal 5, *People are like that in New York*:

A: HAD I BEEN . . . had I been . . . anything OTHER than that . . . I
         could've fallen and they would have stepped OVER me . . . Or
         perhaps ON me. You know cause that's the way people in New
         York ARE.

We have already discussed most of the evaluation present in this
portion when discussing Proposal 4 above. Only the last line, *You
know cause that's the way people in New York are*, distinguished
Proposal 4B from Proposal 5. Not only is this a story about how
people are not *really nice*, the speaker puts it forward as a story of
how people in New York really are. The stress on *are* and the appeal
to the audience with *you know* both highlight this sentence.

C insists in her Proposal 6, *The speaker is an inept subway rider*,
that the speaker may deviate negatively from the norm of American
adults. Implicit in her question is the notion that the speaker's story
may well be an account of her incompetence as a subway rider.

A: Didn't you used to grab the strap in the subway?

is C's devastating phrasing of her proposal. The locution *grab the strap* is, itself, an indication of C's mastery over the subway idiom and probably over the subway itself. Her use of the doubting negative interrogative *didn't you used to* gives the impression that C has thought very little of the speaker's whole story, since she might not have fallen at all if she had ben a competent traveler—a proper, responsible adult.

The speaker's answer to C's charge of incompetence is to move back into the story proper, return to the moment of fainting, and evaluate the altered perceptions she experienced while losing consciousness. First she answers C's question:

A: I . . . was just saying . . . I . . . yeah . . . But I was in . . . standing in the center of the car, holding onto the center POLE . . . and I just slid down the pole.

Since she was holding onto the pole, evaluated by increased stress and repetition of the key word *pole*, she did not need to grab the strap even though she normally did. Having re-established herself as a competent subway rider, she presents her last proposal, 7, *Fainting warps perception*, to re-establish herself as a competent storyteller:

A: A-nd uh- . . . it was funny because . . . in my HEAD . . . I said . . . my AWAREness was such . . . that . . . that that I said to myself . . . gee, well there's a PERson over there falling DOWN. And that person was me.

Here a variety of devices are present: the familiar heightened stress on important words; redundancy of expression of important information that involves her consciousness (*in my head, my awareness was such*); and as in Proposal 1, reported speech. This time the reported speech is closer to direct than to indirect discourse—the *gee, well* which precedes the substance of the sentence is a much more forceful and immediate way of noting that she commented on herself fainting than the earlier *I remember saying to myself*. Unlike the earlier rendition of the story, the fainting itself is curiously muted: *and I just slid down the pole*.

Although the speaker does not comment on why she thought she experienced something impossible (i. e. watching herself faint), she understands that her audience can interpret the marked evaluation on perception to mean that she merely *perceived* herself as experiencing something impossible. The expression *my awareness was such*, with its formal, scientific ring, perhaps makes this point most clearly. The external remark *it was funny because* shows that she agrees that what she perceived was odd. It also has the effect of eliminating any lingering remains of Proposal 1, that this is the story of a frightening experience. Proposal 7 suggests that this is the story of an interesting experience.

B accepts the proposal by saying:

B: It's weird

and the speaker accepts the acquiescence and closes the negotiation by answering:

A: OK, that was . . . that experience.

After detailing a number of proposals, and looking at many minute aspects of the texts and declaring them to be "evaluative," it seems fair to ask if everything can be though of as evaluative. Can a case be made that every part of a text contains a proposal of what the story is all about? In light of these reasonable questions, let us look briefly at the missing proposal, *Men Are All Like That*. This proposal could have been made during the long narrative portion in which the speaker is recounting her interaction with the policeman:

A: He came over, . . . and asked what was wrong, and he asked me just
        two questions. Are you pregnant? . . . To which I said no. I mean they
        . . . like he was told that I had fainted . . . And uh . . . uh he said . . .
        in a very embarrassed kind of way, do you have your period now, . . .
        And I said no . . . A-nd he said OK, and he sat me down, and they got
        an ambulance.

B apparently expected the policeman's embarrassed questioning of the speaker's "biologic functioning" to be of some import. Her chuckle, as if getting the point, when the speaker says *he was told that I had fainted,* becomes a full laugh with the question *Do you have your period, now?* But the speaker ploughs right on with her detailing of events.

Jefferson (1979) suggests that "tellers can propose and recipients accept that a response was premature, that there is more story to come, and that upon a next completion point, recipients have another opportunity to respond via their corrected understanding of the story" (p. 220). This comment is made in reference to a conversational fragment in which the speaker *explicitly* corrects a recipient's misunderstanding. What we have in this story and in some others we have looked at is an *implicit* correction of a misunderstanding in which the speaker strongly underevaluates an event or situation potentially worth evaluating and hurries on with the next part of the story.

In this case, the conversation with the policeman, normally a highly charged event, is reported in a very matter-of-fact way. One event follows another: *he said . . . I said* are events phrased in a muted form, indistinguishable from unevaluated events as *he sat me down* and *they got an ambulance. He asked his question in a very embarrassed kind of way* has some evaluative force, as does *like he was told that I had fainted* but somehow the force is lost, dissipated by the combination of the soft voice in which she details the events and the rather monotonous chain of simple declarative sentences in the past tense filled with details of a rather pedestrian sort. A story about how a policeman asks a woman embarrassing personal questions he could never ask a man is the kind of story which has very strong narratable qualities, especially in a group of somewhat feminist women. That she did not choose to make *men are all like that* or *Man's inhumanity to woman* one of her proposals, is perhaps due to a possible plan to make a more global and important point by asserting that subway travel is inhuman and even "dehumanizing." But this is the most idle sort of speculation. We cannot know what the speaker had in mind, by choosing not to do something which might never have occurred to her to do.

3.8 Conclusion

Some people have asked if these stories are anomalous texts. After all, not every story is so full of comments and interruptions, negotiations and discussion. However, real texts, collected from real speakers, are almost invariably complex. Stories told in unstructured conversation are often discussed, corrected, edited, amplified. The point of a story often changes in the course of narration, and afterward, even beyond the confines of the particular conversation in which it was told. Any point which is accepted as the point by all members of a group has to satisfy several constraints: the story must illustrate the point; the point must be of a narratable sort; and the point must be of interest to the members of the community who generate and receive it.

4

The World Evoked by American Stories

4.0 Introduction

If stories are complex, storytellers are that much more complex; if the storyworlds built by tellers in their stories are complex, the everyday world in which those tellers live and talk and interact with one another is that much more complex. Having looked at the linguistic structure of American stories and dealt a bit with the relationship between stories and embedding conversations, let us now turn our attention towards the tellers of those stories and more specifically towards the system of notions, ideas, concepts, and values which taken together form our common world view. The aim of the present enterprise, then, is not mainly to explain the stories which have been analyzed to "find out what they mean" but rather to explore the world which they evoke.

4.1 Method of Analysis

Taking as a point of departure those aspects of the stories which the narrators have evaluated as especially important, I will begin by inquiring what is interesting about them. I will ask that question in order to elicit from myself what is the most obvious, automatic, trite thing to say about "friends," for example, or "food." And then I follow where the discussion leads. Some constructs will appear very rich, while others may be exhausted sooner. In general, discussions will grow longer as the chapter unfolds, because earlier elaborations of some constructs are available for further exploration. Not every facet of every issue can be discussed since the very basic presuppositions underlying American life are the focus of attention. Some will be hit upon repeatedly, however. The discussion will largely focus on the "individual," his "needs," "choices," social responsibilities and his interpersonal relationships.

Travel from one construct to another is accomplished by means of an associative chain. It is not really possible to talk about the "rights" of the individual without speaking, too, of his "responsibilities" or to inquire into "courage" without considering why one should not act like a "coward." I will try to be as self-referential as possible, looking at what I have just put forward as obvious, and examining to see what sorts of obvious statements can be made about that. I shall not try to come up with "new insights." Indeed, the success of this venture depends on the lack of novelty about the information unearthed. If I say something new, something controversial, I would probably be expressing my own opinions and idiosyncratic, although culturally constrained, point of view. Since the aim is to get at the most globally acceptable remarks, the more conventional and stereotypic the attitude expressed, the more it reflects commonly held attitudes.

Those attitudes need to be explored, to be expounded, because they are commonplaces for Americans; but for those to whom Americans are "foreigners," these clichés may well be very strange. Cultural differences are most strikingly observed in the most commonplace ideas about life. From time to time I will use short excerpts from a particularly American genre of popular psychology and sociology books—the "how to run your life and know how to feel and relate to other people" books. These books are guides for living life "right," having the appropriate feelings, and expressing them in the best way to be "a winner in the life game." (T. I. Rubin, 1967) Most of these books discuss friendship or marriage but all take as their point of departure the individual person who is isolated and feeling helpless. Their advice is intended to help him experience himself as competent, capable of "having relationships" and feeling strong and "autonomous" although accepting that the "truth" of the human condition is that each of us is, quite deeply, alone.

The titles of the quoted books encode a wealth of culturally salient information:

Actualizations: You Don't Have to Rehearse to be Yourself by Stewart Emery (1978)

A Guide to Successful Marriage by Albert Ellis and Robert A. Harper (1977)

Friends: The Power and Potential of the Company You Keep by Jerry Gillies (1976)

Creative Intimacy: How to Break the Patterns that Poison Your Relationships by Dr. Jerry A. Greenwald (1975)

The Adjusted American: Normal Neuroses in the Individual and Society by Snell Putney and Gail J. Putney (1964)

How to Take Charge of Your Life by Mildred Newman and Bernard Berkowitz (1978)

The Winner's Book by Theodore Issac Rubin, M.D. (1967)

A proper American, it seems, is adjusted, in charge of his life, successfully married, and a winner who knows how to be angry, have friends, be free of poisonous personal relationships, and is himself.[1]

The purpose of using these "how to" books is not to substantiate that what I say is the truth about the way which human beings are, but rather to demonstrate that the presuppositions about the way the world is and the way people are which are stumbled on as I follow the threads of my intuition are not really personal statements. Well meaning, serious people who are trying to explain how the world is use exactly the same sorts of statements and rely upon exactly the same kinds of presuppositions about the world that

---

[1] Throughout this discussion, unless I am specifically dealing with women, I will use the male forms, "he," "his" etc. In part the English language still demands that we do so. To use "She/he," "his/hers" and the other compromise forms, merely makes the "solution" too obvious. there is a deeper issue here as well--the "unmarked" person is male, just as he is healthy, of normal intelligence, competent in common living skills, etc., as shall be developed in Chapter Five below.

we are trying to track down. For the same reason, sometimes I will use a line from a popular song, a proverb or cliché. These are so "true," so "ordinary," that we hardly notice that they carry with them and evoke little pieces of a very complex and extraordinary everyday reality.

Clearly, considering the enormity of the task, I will not be able to put together a very complete picture of that reality. This discussion of cultural constructs should be taken as only a demonstration of a method for using story materials as an entry into the cluster of basic interwoven ideas which lies behind and supports our daily lives.

I cannot prove that there is only a limited number of "interesting" things to talk about in a given culture, but that may well be the case. In working through various propositions from the Adequate Paraphrases and the proposals for meaning from "Fainting on the Subway," previously mentioned constructs will often re-emerge. In general, when that happens, the discussion will take a new direction so that as many associative pathways as possible can be explored. In the last section of the chapter when we turn to "The Robbery" the aim will be to demonstrate as far as possible the redundant nature of these explorations and to sketch out how the discussion might have developed had those paths been explored earlier. A good deal of redundancy is to be expected in this sort of analysis since a tremendously extensive set of beliefs about the world would have little utility in structuring our experience.

In general, as has often been said, stories are about deviations from expected norms, although they often function as well to confirm the correctness of preconceived ideas about the way the world is. This fits in very well with our notions of the need for coherence and consistency in the world. Stories give us information about the way the world is—either how we expect it to be or how it differs from our model. The analysis of stories and speakers' motivations which is being presented here similarly depends upon an assumed need for human behavior to be predictable—to conform to norms. My premise is that without the ability to model the interests and world-knowledge of others, human beings would have no idea of what to tell a story about. Indeed, in an incoherent universe, stories and other forms of communication would have little purpose. (See discussion throughout this chapter for analysis of some of the presuppositions rampant in this paragraph!)

4.2 *Fainting on the Subway*

Let us now look closely at the proposals for meaning of "Fainting on the Subway" put forward in Section 3.7. We will list them once again to refresh our memories, and then we will examine the presuppositions behind these proposals in the order in which they are presented.

4.2.1 *In Defense of this Method of Cultural Analysis*
Using American stories to tell the American story is an ambitious enterprise. Through the wide-ranging, almost uncontrolled expansion of the points of the stories which we have been looking at, we may find some American answers to some important (American) questions:

> Why are these ambitious questions?
> Why is it all right to be "ambitious"?
> Why do we want to know the answers to questions?
> Why is it important to know things in general?
> How do we select what is worth knowing?
> What is important? What is unimportant?
> What are people like?
> How do different sorts of people differ from one another?
> How should people behave?
> How is the world organized?
> Is the world organized?
> What is the world like?

It is fair to ask at this point why one would look to intuitive free association, starting from the points of conversational stories for the answers: Why base conclusions on the clichés of quack media healers instead of on the research of responsible psychologists, sociologists, and anthropologists?

And there are several answers to these questions.

In the first place, there has been surprisingly little work done on "world view" of developed Western cultures. Or, rather, there has been a great deal of work done but it is not called "science," it is called "philosophy," "aesthetics," and "ethics." Rediscovering "truth" in strings of clichés and best-selling advice allows us to examine it more critically and to discover the interconnections among basic values. We do not reach "absolute primitives" by this method; we reach a set of mutually supporting and defining constructs. These can then be isolated and the formal relationships among the elements specified.

Of course social scientists have done a great deal of detailed work on specific issues and problems in Western societies, particularly on American society. A close examination of both popular and academic psychological, historical, sociological, and anthropological literature reveals, however, that the "experts'" analyses and arguments are built upon exactly the sort of presuppositions which we are trying to reach. Often analysts will stand on one presupposition to examine others, just as I am doing. In this study, there is an examination of the shifting nature of these presuppositions in both the form of the analysis and its presentation.

Clearly, I am a relativist—of the worst kind from the point of view of those who believe in universals, objectivity, explanation, *the* facts. But when we consult the experts, we find no more objectivity in their texts than elsewhere, no matter how the presentation may bristle with formulas, charts, statistics, complex syntax, or technical jargon. And though it is seldom admitted publicly (except in the pages of the *London Times Literary Supplement*), social scientists often find that the scholarship of "foreign" colleagues provides revealing insights into the authors' cultural background as well as possibly adding to the understanding of the subject matter at hand. In this book, the author's cultural background, although not her idiosyncratic experiences or viewpoints, *is* the subject matter.

Let us now turn to the stories themselves once again to see what can be learned about their tellers' world view from one American analyst's naive cultural exploration.

4.3 *"Fainting on the Subway"*

Since it is perhaps the most complex story treated, as well as the most recent, let us begin our exploration of American world view by examining, in turn, each of the Proposals for Meaning from "Fainting on the Subway." The aim is not to explain the story, nor to come to a decision of what that story was "really about" or "really accomplishing." Rather each of the proposals themselves shall function as mini-texts to be expanded. Many of the points explored in the expansion of these proposals will surface again in analyses of subsequent stories. the proposals are discussed in the order in which they occurred in the telling.

Proposals for Meaning

1. Fainting on the subway is frightening.
2A. Personal problems in the past are important.
2B. Personal problems in the present are even more important.
3. Rush hour is as terrible as living through Nazi concentration camp horrors.
4A. People are nice.
4B. People aren't *really* nice—they are bigots.
5. People are like that in New York.
6. Speaker is an inept subway rider.
7. Fainting warps perception.

Fainting on the Subway is Frightening

Why is fainting frightening? and why is something frightening narratable? Fainting is frightening because it involves a loss of consciousness and hence a loss of control. If we are not in control, we cannot protect ourselves from danger, but are helpless, reduced to the status of children who must be cared for. Indeed, when the speaker faints, she finds herself in such a helpless state. She ceases to be in control of her own life but becomes someone to be sat down, taken hither and yon, asked questions, and left to just stay in a hospital. Not to be in control, to be unable to make decisions for ourselves, puts us at the mercy of other people which is extremely frightening. An adult trusts only himself to know what to do, and, ultimately, to act in his own best interests. Fear in general is an interesting topic for a story, because it is painful and confusing. People are supposed to be happy and unafraid, yet fear is often justified. Knowing when to be afraid is one mark of an adult. Tension can be created in stories which involve fear because there is always a question of whether that fear will be shown to be justified; fearing unnecessarily makes us children; not fearing when there are grounds for fear is a sign of madmen or fools.

Personal Problems in the Past Are Important
In the story the speaker details a number of factors which added together produced a state of tremendous emotional pressure. But why detail these circumstances at all? No doubt she felt it necessary to make it abundantly clear that she was not the sort of person who normally faints; she usually functioned properly unless there was a compelling reason to do otherwise. But why are such personal problems of interest? Americans find information about people to be endlessly fascinating. Even Europeans, closer to us culturally than many other peoples, are often struck by how often Americans will offer details of emotional or personal situations to even a casual acquaintance.

We value openness, and the closer the individual is to us, the more interesting his personal affairs. But, why? Perhaps because the individual is all-important. Concern with the individual is the center of our political, judicial, religious and economic philosophies: we bring our children up to be able to act independently. Our heroes are men who stand against the crowd. We have few set rules of conduct, of how to be, but many meta-rules of each finding his own way. Information about other people's difficulties gives us information about how to act in our own lives; seeing how others deal with adversity gives us a model for dealing with difficulties of our own; and learning of someone else's hardships and failures makes us feel more "normal," less inadequate, since we know that we ourselves cannot deal perfectly with every situation which comes along either. An adult must be strong, able to manage for himself, and each of us knows that we cannot. This is a dilemma, a problem facing us because of our deepest feelings about the way adults are and how they ought to be. We are very concerned with our own individuality, and yet we are preoccupied with being popular—we must each be unique, but not odd, different. Someone who confides to us his personal problems makes us feel trusted. It is a way of baring the neck. By discussing her problems, the speaker in "Fainting on the Subway" simultaneously announces that she is vulnerable, and that she is unafraid; that she is "normal" and that she is "unique." One way that her recital declares her to be normal is in the exact choice of details selected to show her distress: she had no air; she had insufficient room; she had not eaten; she had no job, and, presumably, little money—all needs which we take to be basic and human.

As one popular psychology book puts it: "Whatever else man may be, he is first of all an animal with certain requirements for oxygen, tolerable temperatures, water, sleep, food and so forth." (Putney and Putney, 1964: 22)

If those requirements are not met, a human cannot survive and thus an adult cannot behave like an adult. That needs are not always met may mitigate the responsibility of an individual to perform adequately. Although an adult must be strong, competent, always in control, this is not possible if her basic needs are not met. This argues for a physical and materialistic view of the world: being deprived of "needs" is an excuse for not behaving as we should (see Benedict [1967] and Goffman [1961] for extended discussion of the "needs" of human beings in Japan and the United States respectively and the results of depriving them of those "needs. "

Personal Problems in the Present Are Even More Important
In proposing that her problems in the past have ramifications for the present, the speaker was relying upon the audience's understanding of the nature of "needs" and the explanatory power of

personal history. In addition she marshalls the very significant power of the immediate experience of an individual. If past problems are fascinating, present ones are that much more so. By stating that she is still unable to ride a subway alone, a totally normal and everyday act for many people, she is relying on a group of cultural presuppositions to carry the force of her comments. Each individual has a unique history, and events and experiences in a person's past can account for personality and behavior in the present. Unlike many other people who ascribe the way a person is to the events surrounding his birth or the nature of one's ancestors, we have a causal and historical explanation for the present state of an individual. By bringing the effects of this experience into the present, the speaker is bringing it closer to her audience—insisting that this is not merely a story about the past, but is, in fact, a story about the present and an explanation of why she is less than totally competent at carrying out the comings and goings of everyday life.

Rush Hour is Dehumanizing: Like a Concentration Camp
We may ask why a story which could stand as an illustration of horrors equal to those of the concentration camp might be narratable. Since stories of atrocities are not necessarily to be found in all cultures, we cannot assume that it is "human nature" to be interested in atrocity; yet for us nothing is more tellable. Why? To deprive someone of his needs is to treat him like an animal. An animal is without individuality, at the command of his instincts, without the faculties of language or thought. To treat a man as an animal is to make him become an animal. The worst fate which can befall a man is to become like a beast; and the worst pain one person can inflict on another is to reduce him to the animal.

Nazi concentration camps and, presumably, New York subways, epitomize the way the world should not be and thus a story about these matters is an illustration of a strong deviation from a proper world.

People Are Nice

Stories are often built around deviations from expected norms of behavior, of "the way it is supposed to be," as can clearly be seen in Proposal 3. However, stories can also be moral tales of right conduct, or tales which illustrate the proper and the true. People are supposed to be "nice" and help each other in difficult situations. This type of kindness toward strangers is built upon the very strong democratic and pragmatic notion that each individual should be treated equally especially when he cannot help himself—after all, anyone might be in a similar position someday. Whether stranger, friend, or kinsman, someone who needs help must be aided. In American culture, the primary bond between individuals is by virtue of their common humanity; not, as in many cultures, between those who have formal relationships with one another by reason of family, clan, or social position, although such ties are, of course, recognized and are very important.

We are more alone than is possible for someone with closer ties to imagine. Friends, family, teachers, religious leaders—all are temporary relations at best. American "how to" books extol the importance of the individual freeing himself from ties which are too binding, too restrictive.

To view all your friendships as temporary, as unfeeling as this may seem to you, will actually enhance the quality of those relationships, make them more human. For our lives are temporary things, and to cling, to hold on, is foolish as well as self-defeating. (Gillies, 1976, p. 200)

Any given person may be a potential "friend" and any given situation may be one in which one makes the kind of ties which render us less alone. Being "nice" is a way of keeping our options open. By helping and being helpful to people regardless of the degree of relationship we have to them, we have the possibility of developing a relationship to them. However, we must not allow ourselves to be overwhelmed by our desire for companionship:

If you are a healthy and mature individual, you will acknowledge that other people are necessary to your growth and existence. If you are a needy, dependent individual, you will be desperately seeking others to reaffirm you, to love you, and however many people become a part of your life it will never be enough. (Gillies, 1976, p. 148)

Thus, there is a basic and often painful conflict between the need for friendship, ties, community, and the very strong pressure to be an individual who is self-contained and responsible only to himself.

People Are Not Nice
The speaker counters the proposal that "people are nice" by insisting that they were not really nice, but were nice to her only because she was the kind of person anyone would be nice to without having to be a nice person through and through. This comment is based on the assumption that it is possible *to act* one way, and *to be* another. Being is rooted in what is really felt not what is merely done. Thus it is possible to know someone's true nature apart from his behavior. This is quite a novel notion to many non-Americans, who wonder how one can know this true nature exists, if there is no manifestation of it in behavior.

That people may be one way "inside" and show a very different face to the world is a psychological commonplace. The "outer" face is felt to be less genuine, less true in important ways. By acting in accordance with the outer face and not the inner face a person does himself an injustice and ultimately others as well who are not relating to the *real* person. This real person exists however and is most readily accessible in moments of great emotion when the true person may be liberated from the falsely behaving person. American psychotherapy is based on getting to know and liberating the true person through techniques which induce, encourage, permit, and reward outbursts of anger, pain, rage, and sadness which are more genuine than the rational, intellectual, controlled, socially pleasant reactions which are normally encouraged and required.

This deep, emotional, true self is always lurking and it is the true self, the one which emerges when there is a threat to the individual. It is therefore imperative for people to keep tabs on the true selves of others—because in an emergency the true self will be present, complete with the real feelings and the rational outer self will be gone. When the speaker insists that the subway riders were not really nice she refers to the knowledge every adult must have that the world is not as it may seem, people are not as they seem, not even as they behave. People are what they would be under the most trying circumstances. When you can trust someone "when the chips are down" you can trust him. It is important to be able to distinguish between what a person may be like under pleasant conditions from what he might be like when things get difficult.

People Are Like That in New York
Why are New York stories interesting? New York and New Yorkers are quintessentially "other" for most Americans, including New Yorkers. Anything can happen in New York, and it will probably be more exciting, more interesting, and worse than anything which happens anywhere else (unlike Texas, where things are only bigger and better). Even a story documenting how New Yorkers are ordinary folks who can do a stranger a kindness is narratable because such a story is an atypical New York story. The deviant case is always interesting; and New York is a deviant part of America, in marked contrast to the Midwest, which is the American norm.

Why is the deviant so fascinating? The everyday so humdrum? The exception is so exciting because it presents new possibilities; shows new vistas, gives an indication of a world in which the traditional encumbrances are not felt. The different, the deviant, the exotic is interesting because it represents a type of freedom. The individual experiences himself as more fully individualized, more in touch with inner capabilities, unfettered by tradition, *free*. Freedom unfettered, independent, able to experience the possibilities of the world, to understand its complexity. These are all self-evident goods. Therefore, we are always fascinated by the deviant, although often frightened and disapproving of it. We take great pains to try to establish the "norm," if only to show how *we* do not fit it. (Even the discussion of evaluative functioning and cultural salience is built on the idea of norms and the power of deviance from norms.)

Speaker an Inept Subway Rider
A story of ineptness is fully narratable because adults are supposed to be competent, to be able to take care of themselves, and to be knowledgeable about their environment and the ways of managing everyday aspects of daily life. Failing to control the environment, being unable to "cope," is shameful. Difficulties with the environment, other people, or even with oneself, can be dealt with, can be overcome, but only with knowledge. Knowledge is power and control. Adults are knowledgeable; children are ignorant. The most stigmatized in our society, the mentally retarded, are pitied and despised because they alone among humans can never be *adult*, never be *competent*, never *know*.

One requirement of adults is that they manage their lives. Our lives are a kind of work to be done well, like any other type of work. To live incompetently is synonymous with living wrongly. An incompetent person, like any other stigmatized person, makes normals uncomfortable and his presence in the collective is barely tolerated. A person who is unable to DO is excluded from life because his presence is unbearable and because a person who suffers is wrong. Suffering in itself is a sign of wrongbeing. (See Goffman [1963] for a discussion of "stigmatized" and "normal" persons. These are his terms.)

We live in a hierarchical system of inherited prestige and power, a system in which relatively few privileged persons share in the tremendous wealth and policy-making institutions of the world's richest nation. Yet our professed belief is in the equality of all men before the election officials who control the ballot box, before the police and judges who administer the laws, before the laws of chance and fortune, and before God himself. In fact, we have no alternative but to maintain that all men have equal chances of becoming the election official, policeman, or judge, though we temper this equality by insisting that "each man gets what he deserves" through the workings of chance and the movements of the Lord.

By postulating that only those who deserve to get rewarded with the good things of life, we attempt to combine two obvious and irreconcilable "truths"—everyone is equally entitled to wealth, power, and good fortune, but not everyone ends up with an equal share. Those who don't end up on the top of the heap obviously don't deserve to. One does not deserve to succeed if one is guilty; therefore, failure to make money, have political power, or even good health is a punishment for some unspecifiable wrongdoing on the part of the individual. Faced with the unavoidable fact that some rich or powerful people are not morally pure, we assume that those people suffer, too. They must feel guilty and be unable to truly enjoy their ill-gotten gains. Unable to look at themselves in the mirror, they are in pain, too, which proves their sinfulness and preserves the integrity of the "suffering equals sin" system.

Since one gets what one deserves, people who are suffering are getting their due. Suffering equals sinfulness, and sinfulness is necessarily accompanied by feelings of guilt which are themselves painful. Psychoanalysis and the Judaeo-Christian religions both operate on this unhappy principle. Political and financial power is concentrated rightly in the hands of those who are not themselves oppressed since an oppressed person is guilty of suffering, at the very least, and is therefore unworthy of having any political power or asserting himself forcefully enough to demand that his unequal lot be improved. The oppressors are less compromised by their participation in an oppressive situation than the oppressed. Those in authority are "more equal" than their social inferiors; the elite has proven its worthiness to rule by the mere fact of having succeeded in being in command. If it were not worthy, it would not have succeeded. The stigmatized, therefore, can be seen as subversive as well as immoral. They undermine the system of political control by their very helplessness and the fact that we must accept the fact that their fate is not, in fact, their fault. We know that the unfortunate may well be innocents, people like ourselves whose plight is not a punishment for wrongdoing but merely an accident of fate, something which could happen to anyone. Those who cannot DO stand at the center of a complex set of mutually exclusive, deeply held beliefs which are very close to the core of our thoughts about the way the world is—how it makes sense.

A world which makes no sense is considered unbearably painful. Anthropology, cognitive and interpersonal psychology, even physics and chemistry depend upon deeply held beliefs about the coherence of the universe. Societies attempt to structure the world for tis members, much as a creature's sensory apparatus acts to arrange the stimulus from the outer world into patterns which can be processed. Children are seen to be structuring their world as they grow and learn—autistic children, however, may suffer from an inability to structure sensory input and therefore live in a world which is incoherent and thus overwhelming, frightening, and paralyzing. The quest for scientific knowledge is said to spring from a similar need to make an otherwise intolerably complex and inchoate world into a whole in which it is possible to be safe because it is possible to know, and to understand which causes lead to which results. An organism which cannot predict, we are told by psychologists, cannot survive. We believe in predicting; we plan, we compare the past to the future using the present as a bridge between the events which we believe have happened and those we are sure will happen. To be disoriented, to be unable to understand, to be unable to create meaningful patterns is perhaps the worse fate which can befall a person because a person who is disorganized *knows* that he is disorganized and cannot function. At the bottom of this discomfiture is the belief that people are by nature conscious beings who must be in control of their environment. To be at the mercy of uncontrollable forces is unbearably destructive for the individual because they render him helpless and thus unhappy.

Being happy is, of course, a self-evident good. *The Adjusted American*, defines happiness as *the emotional state that accompanies need satisfaction.* (Putney and Putney, 1964, p. 16) While most of us would probably define happiness somewhat more in terms of enjoyment, not needing anything, but also feeling good about what is happening, happy is what people are supposed to be, what they have a right to be—at least some of the time—if they are living correctly. Indeed, since people are supposed to be happy, not being happy is a sign that things are not as they should be. Other people observing someone being unhappy may feel compelled to find out what is wrong and try to change the situation so that the unhappy person re-enters the normal and desirable state of happiness. Therefore, failing to be happy when there is no reason not to be happy is actually not proper behavior since other people might have to act in order to change the situation and the person's mood from an unpleasurable to a pleasurable one. This is one reason why there is so much emphasis on smiling. Smiling people signal that they are happy, there is nothing wrong which anyone else should do anything about ("When you're smiling, the whole world smiles with you").

Naturally, there are a number of assumptions involved in statements such as *people would want to do something about unhappiness to change it to happiness.* First of all, it must be understood that people are capable of acting individually to change things and that there is a positive obligation on the individual to be helpful (i. e. effect positive change) whenever possible. This ties in with pitching in in an emergency, or helping a stranger who looks lost find his way. Since people need people and any person can extend help to any other person, one of the best ways to make someone else happy is to be friendly, i. e. act as a friend would under the circumstances, although the individuals concerned may not actually be in a friendship relationship to one another. Since friends are pleased to be with one another, a big smile is one of the surest ways of making a stranger feel at home, or someone in distress feel better, because it is clear that he is "among friends" whether with friends or perfect strangers.

Someone who remains unhappy—and fails to react to being cheered up by acting happy—despite the efforts of others to make him feel better, has to have a very strong reason for remaining gloomy. People have the capacity to change their own moods as well as to bring about change in others and to fail to help yourself and continue to be unhappy and thus force others to continue trying to make you happy is unreasonable behavior. Since the individual is supposed to do for himself, to fail to do so and to force other people to keep doing for you is the worst sort of "manipulative behavior." It is actually a form of shirking work since the unhappy person may be forcing others to do what he refuses to do for himself.

The aim of psychotherapy and other forms of psychological counseling is to help people be happy, often by refusing to allow them to continue to manipulate others—because once the individual knows what he is doing and how he is actually responsible for his own distress he will have no choice but to get happy. It will then be clear that he is doing as much work in remaining unhappy and getting others to do for him as he would have to do for himself were he to take charge of his life. Each person is responsible for his own life and for everything which happens in it and has the power to change for the better and thus the happier at any time he is willing to do the work of getting healthy. If you actually have to work as hard to be unhappy, and have to be guilty about being unhappy and shirking your work, you might as well give up being unhappy and be happy since it is no more effort—it doesn't cost you any more. And a proper person would obviously rather be happy than unhappy if he does not have to "pay more" for it.

There is no justification for a tragic vision of the world; if you are unhappy it is because you want to be unhappy—the world is, at worst, a neutral place and you make of it what you want to make of it. If you are unhappy, it is your own fault; if you feel yourself less than other people, a loser in the game of life, then it is your own fault and no one can help you but you can help yourself if your are willing to face pain (i. e. be courageous) to pay for your previous unhappiness.

Fainting Warps Our Perception of Reality
Altered perceptions are narratable because they suggest that the world may be somewhat different than we perceive it, or, at least, that we cannot always trust the evidence of our own senses. And if not our own senses, then what can we trust? Not the elders, not religion, not tradition, not fate; unlike many other peoples we rely upon none of these. Science? But science is built upon proof by

experimentation, which itself is founded upon the ultimate authority: confirmation by the senses. If seeing is not believing, what can be believed?

We all know that it is impossible to be in two places at once. A story which says that someone experienced being in two places at once is clearly of interest. Adults know that the universe is rational and for every apparently aberrant event there is a rational explanation. Even when we perceive something which is patently impossible, we know that there must be some explanation somewhere in the known and knowable world. The material world is all that exists, and man can control his own world and be *safe* in the world not prey to childish fears and ignorant misconceptions when he knows the simple physical laws of the universe.

Safety is a basic need of human beings. A child must be protected by its mother in order to live; a society must protect its members and give them the security they need in order to survive. Children must be taught very carefully that physical situations may be hazardous and that the world is unsafe. Knowing how to cross the street, how to light a match, how to get in and out of a canoe might save a child's life. Fire safety, electrical hazards and the like are important. Inadequate wiring in a hotel causes more concern than the lack of a view or other aesthetic considerations. Overloaded circuits, naked wires, and high currents are unnerving because you never can tell when an accident will occur and one must plan ahead to avoid danger.

Our world is a physical world; physical dangers are important and real because they cause harm, real harm—to our bodies. Emotions, social relations, are less vulnerable, less important, less real. Aesthetics are a mere pleasant aspect of life and in no way commensurate with harsh, physical realities. Out of the body experiences, trance states, even deep religious rapture are definitely suspect because they are not real. We know that we have a body and it cannot levitate, it cannot be in two places at once, it cannot transcend the physical and operate in another realm. There is no other realm. We may have experiences which lead us to believe that we are experiencing another way of being. In fact, the spiritual is one of the needs of human beings since it provides a kind of coherence for phenomena we cannot otherwise classify (i. e. control) but no adult should take it too seriously, should sacrifice his own life (or worse the lives of those who depend on him) for otherworldly aims.

The speaker acknowledges that she experienced herself as being out of her body and that her experience is reportable because it is so clearly not the way life is. But she underwent this experience for perfectly understandable reasons. Since she did not in fact believe that she had actually seen herself but merely *thought* that she had, she managed to bring into play all of the power of our feelings about the physical world. Sending a double message, an ambiguous signal, she stated simultaneously that listeners should be interested in what happened because it was impossible and value and accept her as one of themselves for knowing it to be impossible.

4.4 *"Eating on the New York Thruway"*

Turning from "Fainting on the Subway" with its very complex negotiation structure and many points to the simpler "Eating on the New York Thruway," reveals many similarities in the cultural constructs underlying both stories.

A number of aspects of the American's world must be dealt with in connection with this story in detail: food, a physical necessity of life; friends and the demands of friendship, social necessities of life; and competence and autonomy, two overwhelming necessities for successful human living. Each of these very large areas is suggested by the story in some way: food is the theme which introduces the story and which ties the story in with the previous discourse, while matters of friendship and competence arise from consideration of the behavior of the characters in the story itself. Friendship as a theme to be explored arises because of the relationship between the two women, Carol and Livia, while competence is suggested by the problems involving the coke and the restaurant employees.

A Story about Food

Carol introduces the topic of food at the very beginning of the telling when she announces her story to be *about water or coke* (Clause 33-34). Food is one of the pleasant necessities of life—eating communally is enjoyable and there is a wide diversity of foods good and tasty to eat.

For Americans, food is normally a safe topic of talk. Different eating habits are matters of interest, and though people are often categorized by their eating habits they are seldom morally condemned for them. We are usually pleased with what we eat and are willing to experiment and try other foods, although there are some foods we do not eat. In common with most peoples we are not omnivores. We find people who eat insects, worms, grubs snakes, cats, dogs, or some wild birds (among other foods) are nearly unpeople, as are those who eat their meat raw. Foods we do not like may be disgusting but eaters of such foods are seldom really immoral unless they eat beings with whom we are used to having personal relationships (i.e. household pets and other humans).

Food is one of the necessities of life and eating is one of the primary functions. Other basic activities, such as breathing and sleeping, are not very interesting unless we are discussing how we were unable to accomplish them. Elimination and procreation, on the other hand, are very interesting topics but are taboo to discuss in adult social conversation except in special circumstances. Food is not narratable simply because it is a necessity of life, or because it is something we find interesting but in general, talk about food is considered *safe*. In social interactions it is very useful to have some topics which are interesting to talk about on which everyone has opinions, and on which there can be disagreement without serious social rupture.

Food becomes socially dangerous as a topic when it is linked with one of two other topics: economics or health. Everyone needs to eat, because people must eat to be healthy, and so the notion that some people cannot afford to eat is extremely upsetting. If they cannot afford food then they cannot live properly and not living properly they are not responsible for what they do. Everyone in an equal and fair society should have the necessities of life or something is very very wrong with the working of the system. The system must work or life becomes incoherent and thus impossible.

Depriving someone of food is immoral, although the taste of food and the nature of the food is not so important. Thus, it is right that poor people and people in prison eat unappetizing food, since the taste of food is a pleasure, but it is wrong if people have no food. Without the necessities of life, people die or become like animals.

Some food is not healthy and should not be eaten. Underdone pork is a health hazard, as is potato salad left out in the sun. Unpasteurized milk is also suspect and someone who would knowingly eat such foods is not a proper person. This concern with health and the healthiness of foods spawns a variety of opinions about what is healthy. One way youth rebels is to pick different food as being healthy than their elders and then to berate their parents and other older folks for eating unhealthily. Unpasteurized milk, for example, has moved from -healthy to +healthy, but eating what is healthy is still important.

Water and coke, the two substances which figure prominently in "Eating on the New York Thruway" are two of the most common and innocuous substances (in a non-health food environment). The speaker's assertion that there was a story involving those drinks would fit smoothly into almost any conversation involving food. Had she mentioned "caviar and escargots," instead, there would have been more question as to how this story fit into the ongoing discourse. Since the topic at hand was eating on the Thruway and she mentioned two very common foodstuffs, both easily procured on the highway at rest stops, the story fit easily and in a non-threatening manner into the conversation.

What is This Story Really About?
Having investigated the matter of food a bit, let us now turn our attention to the Adequate Paraphrase of "Eating on the New York Thruway" which we arrived at in Chapter Three.

Carol was "poisoned" by sipping a coke prepared by weird incompetent people who worked at the restaurant on the New York Thruway. She was saved by Livia who had brought along (an otherwise mysterious) gallon of spring water.

Although it may seem a step backwards, the analytic process begins by decomposing the Paraphrase into its component parts. Each proposition can then be explored individually to see where it leads.

The "plot" of the story reduces to two events:

Carol drank a poisoned coke.

Carol was saved by Livia who gave her water to drink.

While the contextualizing information consists of:

The employees of the restaurant who made the coke were weird and incompetent.

The warning against drinking the coke—all of Livia's vague remarks.

That Livia had brought along spring water.

We will begin with the first event:

A Story About Poisoning

Food is supposed to be reliable, safe, predictable, especially in the United States. A coke is the most ordinary of the ordinary, the most American of the American. A coke which is poisoned is a betrayal of one's trust in the system to provide what can reasonably be expected to be forthcoming.

The key word in the last sentence is "reasonably," since some things clearly are "reasonable" and others "unreasonable." The unreasonable can be wished for, hoped for, or prayed for but an adult accepts that there are limits what he can expect to have. The reasonable is a person's due. If he behaves correctly, then he should get what is "reasonably" coming to him. Indeed, since one gets what is coming to one, not getting the reasonably expected is doubly unpleasant: one does not get what one expected and one's worth is measured by what actually happened. What actually happens is more "reasonable" than what did not happen, since the supposedly reasonable would have happened had it been *truly* reasonable. Carol was punished for not knowing what was reasonable. This is a moral tale in that respect—she is educated about the nature of the world and her ideas of the reasonable in relation to food are realigned, uncomfortably. However, her friend acted as a friend should act, and the experience was thus not altogether negative.

About Friendship

In order to understand the force of the core plot (Carol was saved by her friend who gave her some water to drink), we need to investigate what "friends" are like and gain some understanding of how they relate to each other. We must understand, too, why giving a friend a drink of water when she was poisoned by a coke might constitute an act of friendship.

Friends are people who like each other, who accept each other as they are, and who willingly help each other in troubled times and rejoice together in happy times. Friends, above all, "make us feel they really like us, really respect and appreciate us." (Gillies, 1976, p. 13).

Although "a friend is someone who I know will be there when I need him to be there" (Emery, 1978, p. 153) , a real friend, like a good parent, will not be totally supportive:

... won't settle for your being less than [you really] are and kicks you in the ass when the way your being represents a lie about the way you really are. (Emery, 1978, p. 150)

Honesty is the most important aspect of a friendship. In a friendship one must be free to be who one is and to tell the truth no matter if it is hurtful to the other person, but only if such hurting is done for the other person's good.

There are people who, under the guise of honesty, are always telling other people things that barb and hurt them. This is honesty used in the service of vindictiveness; (Rubin, 1967, p. 33)

So, a good friend is helpful and honest and supportive, managing to negotiate successfully the very thin line between helpfulness and hurtfulness when something in the friend's behavior is not as it should be.

But why have friends when juggling needs and honesties is so difficult? Because in a friendship one can be oneself, one need "play the least amount of roles possible" (as noted by L. Buscaglia in Gillies, 1976, p. 165). With friends one can talk; one can share experiences; one can overcome loneliness. People need people:

The more impersonal our society and its institutions become, the more the individual feels alone, alienated and lost. He then lives in a chronically toxic condition. The person adrift in the world with no anchor loses his identity, the meaningfulness of his life and, eventually, his emotional and physical health. (Greenwald, 1975, p. 11)

One solution, according to Greenwald, is to become your own best friend. This solution is clearly rooted in the more ordinary solution to the problem of loneliness: have friends.

Clearly, one has friends because they are *useful*: friends fulfill a human need, not to be alone. Having friends is healthy. Needing to have friends, relying on one's friends heavily, however, is not good. It is in conflict with the healthy individual's ability to be independent and get along fine by himself:

Warning: Beware of the person who sends the message implicit or explicit, "I want someone to take care of me." Chances are he or she lacks inner intimacy and feelings of stability and self-love. (Greenwald, 1976, p. 13)

It is important to *choose* one's friends carefully because:

We invest a lot of time and energy in our friends. Time and energy exist for us in limited quantities, and we can't afford to waste much of either. (Gillies, 1976, p. 13)

It is important to make choices properly because what an individual wants or does can influence events, other people, perhaps the future of the world. Choices made by individuals determine what may happen. Choice is a *fact* and the action of the individual is all important. History revolves around individual figures who made decisions, took chances, perhaps changed the course of future events.

Choice is not only an option for an individual; it is a responsibility. A proper person is one who acts autonomously in his own best interests:

Autonomy means the capacity of the individual to make valid choices of his behavior in light of his needs. To the extent that his choices are limited externally (by coercion) or internally (by normal neurosis or sterile rebellion) the individual is incapable of autonomy. (S. Putney and G. Putney, 1964, p. 10)

An individual who is "incapable of autonomy" is not free. In the opinion of the authors of *The Adjusted American: Normal Neuroses in the Individual and Society* such a person is "neurotic." And ". . . neurosis which inhibits the fulfillment of needs . . . is . . . a threat to physical as well as mental health" (p. 17).

Health functions in this argument as a self-evident good. People who are not capable of choosing correctly and thus protecting their emotional and physical beings are not proper members of society. If they cannot take care of themselves properly they can obviously not take care of others and fulfill their roles as productive persons. The individual is always the most important person in his own life, and one does best by what one cares most about:

In doing for others, we are also involved in doing for self through the personal satisfaction derived from relating to others in this way. Doing for self and doing for others are therefore never mutually exclusive and constantly complement and supplement a continuing human process. (T. I. Rubin, 1976, p. 42)

So, one takes care of one's friends, but they should not *need* to be taken care of. "Taking care of" involves being there, being helpful, and being honest. Doing the supportive thing which helps the other person in his life but doing these things because one *wants* to do them. Friends must both be friends and act towards one another as friends. Unfortunately, these two constraints may come into conflict with one another, since one must *freely* behave as a friend is *constrained* to behave by the force of conventions of friendship. If one is not behaving in accordance with one's *true* feelings, then one is not being a true friend, because with a friend one should be honest; if one is not being honest then the relationship ceases to be safe for either side, since the true feeling might leak out at any time and reveal that the behavior has been a sham. Dishonesty can be devastating to a friendship and all that the friends have invested in the relationship over the years may not be able to save it.

If there are problems or upsets among two or more friends, it may become imperative for all involved to have a talk to try to reach an understanding. Sometimes it may take a number of conversations to straighten things out. Eventually one or both parties to the disagreement might give up trying. In the latter case, the relationship may be considered to be either at an end or else less solid than it had felt before the altercation. Relationships often feel *more* solid, on the other hand, after a process of reconciliation than they had before the difficulty developed.

Explicit communication has great power to build *trust* in a relationship. Trust is overwhelmingly important in relationships in which each party knows that he has the power to end the relationship if it is not pleasing to him and knows, too, that the other partner in the relationship has the same power. Friendships, marriages, business associations, neighbor relationships, and family ties are always threatened by displeasure on the part of any one of the parties involved. The threat that a relationship may be terminated if it is not straightened out puts it into a class of problems demanding immediate attention. Problems are there to be solved; problems in relationships are to be solved by talking things out, expressing your feelings to the other person, being real, uninhibited by social conventions, expectations of being nice, of letting it all hang out.

Until the problem is straightened out, the people involved are unable to relate to each other normally. Merely being nice in a social way is phony; we need to know what the other person really feels because only then can we feel safe, can we rest assured that we are behaving properly towards the other person. If the other is denying the relationship, intending perhaps to break it off, then behaving as if a relationship really existed would be uncomfortable, would make a fool out of the person who believed the other to be truly involved. A commitment by both parties to talk it out, work it through indicates a commitment to continue the relationship, paying for it with the time and energy spent in arguing, explaining, and sharing an upset.

Knowing that the other cares leads to a sense of safety and security. One relaxes; one knows that the other cares also and one has usually learned something about the other in the course of the working it out process. What is learned becomes a token of the worth the relationship since a piece of intimate knowledge about someone else may be used against that person in other arguments.

Once they have established that the relationship will go on, the disputing partners need to agree on the version of the precipitating events they will agree to share so that, should the matter come up again, it will not be a threat to the relationship because all will know what to think of it. A consensus would have been reached. In the course of all the talk about the problem, and the problem relationship, the involved people express their feelings toward each other and about the way things are. When we do so, we find that our "real" emotions are essentially indistinguishable since we feel a common battery of them: pain, anger, sadness, alienation, joy, warmth, insecurity, and so forth. Deep down, then, we are basically all the same. This sympathy and security which develops from feeling at one with the other person leads to a resolution of the original conflict and a strengthening of the relationship itself. Having been through something together and being still willing to continue the relationship has proven that there is something important there after all. Stewart Emery in his book

Actualizations: You Don't Have to Rehearse to be Yourself puts this whole matter nicely:

The truth about you and me is that we have fundamentally similar essences and different realities. The different realities enable the game called relationship to take place. And the experience of the similarity of essence allows the game called relationship to take place without threat. You can have a lot more fun playing the game if you are not worried about the outcome. (Emery, 1978, p. 91)

Once we have discovered our similarity, our essential equality, we need not be afraid of the other but are free to have fun playing the game of relationship. Naturally, when we tire of playing that particular game with that particular partner, the relationship is once again in trouble, because it has stopped being *fun*, being enjoyable, being useful.

Sad as it often seems, friendships do end, and in fact they must end when they are no longer useful. Gillies quotes "Group leader Emily Coleman" as saying:

Make a clean sweep. Trim down your list of friends to those who really inspire you, and you'll find you have time and energy to seek new friends. (Gillies, 1976, p. 197)

Coleman's proposal is predicated on the idea of there being infinite opportunities possible in life. The individual's responsibility is to make the best of his time and resources, to take advantage of as much as possible.

Friendship, then, is almost a kind of property. We can invest time and money in it, expect to get things out of it, and exchange worn out relationships for ones which are better for us. At the core of all of this is an individual trying to stave off isolation, for his health if for no other reason, and attempting simultaneously to "have" as many relationships as possible. Friendships are, by nature, temporary. The individual must choose to have them and choose to continue to have them by agreeing to behave as a friend quite spontaneously. Relationships in general are transitory, freely chosen, and should last as long as they have utilitarian value:

We must let go of our family, our friends, even our life. So long as we cling to life as a permanent possession, it will not be as full as it can be. (Reid quoted in Gillies , 1976, p. 200)

Life, friends, family, it seems should be viewed as *temporary* possessions. Friends are better than family in some respects:

The reason for this is obvious. We choose our friends. (Streamer quoted in Gillies, 1976, p. 210)

Choice emerges over and over again in these discussions as one of the most important aspects of human life.

A Story About Friendship
Let's consider briefly two important inferences easily made from propositions explicitly stated in "Eating on the New York Thruway":

Carol drank a "poisoned coke" (From Propositions 83-84)

Livia, Carol's friend had warned her against all comestibles at the Thruway Restaurant (from Propositions 37-40/43 and 44)

Carol was saved by her friend's giving her water to drink. Both Carol and Livia behaved as proper people. Carol did not heed Livia's advice because she did not understand it, and as an adult, she had to make her own independent decision. Livia behaved properly both by warning Carol against danger and then by offering her the spring water when Carol was in danger. She did not hold it against her friend that Carol had previously ignored her warning. Carol accepted Livia's help, thereby allowing her own distress to be relieved and allowing Livia to act like a friend towards her by helping her out of her difficulties. Both women emerge as proper friends and proper adults.

A Story of Competence

To finish up this discussion of some of the issues raised by aspects of "Eating on the New York Thruway," let' look closely at two highly evaluated propositions in Carol's telling:

The coke was prepared by weird incompetent people (who may have been insane or mentally deficient) [Propositions 61-7/69/70/73]

Livia had brought along a gallon of spring water. [Propositions 39/44.]

The restaurant personnel were *incompetent* and Livia was *competent*.[2] They did not know how to do the simplest thing required of them, while Livia was well prepared for the exigencies of Thruway eating.

Adults are supposed to be competent. They should be able to take care of their own needs, as we have mentioned above, and they must be able to deal adequately with their environment. Without the ability to fend for themselves, people are in danger since each person is alone in the social world. There is no cushion of social or family ties, no dependable world which protects the individual or satisfies his needs. Along with the right to choose and the need to choose to fill his own needs, is the inevitable necessity of taking care of himself in every way.

People ought to do things for themselves and doing can be fun. Some of the more exclusive vacation spots in the United States with guest lists limited to the wealthiest and most socially elite have the most primitive accommodations including ice boxes, no heat, primitive sanitary facilities. Public officials and bank presidents clean their own fish, repair their own gasoline outboard motors and take the car into town for a lube job. Their wives, meanwhile, supervise their own children, iron their own clothes, and make the

---

[2]   There are clearly problems involved in analyzing oneself as a character in a story or as a participant in an interaction. However, as hopefully this analysis will make clear, there are compensatory benefits as well since some aspects of what is involved in the data being analyzed are clearly more accesible to the participants than to more "neutral" observers.

beds in the cabin. At home, these same people insist that their children do chores, even if there are servants to supervise that the dishes are put in the dishwasher properly, or the lawn edges are trimmed correctly. Children wash and clothe themselves at a relatively early age: signs of independent purposeful accomplishments are welcomed and even insisted upon. It is not uncommon for even very small children of under three years to "get themselves organized" in the morning.

"No one's going to do it for you, so you'd better do it yourself" is one of the maxims of daily life and *being able* to do for yourself is a matter of pride and a source of self-worth. Not everyone knows how to fix a car, of course, though it is a source of embarrassment should anyone find that out. Some work may sometimes be substituted for other work which is being opted out of. The substituted work must be at least as difficult, preferably have unpleasant physical associations or pay better. If one or the other of the first two conditions are met, one is not guilty of laziness, irresponsibility, or shirking. If one can use the time to greater financial advantage, then, clearly, one should do the work which pays more over that which pays less even if the less remunerative is something one ought to do. Thus, a woman doctor need not clean her own house since she would make much more money by working than she would spend for a housecleaner. On the other hand, she should certainly garden or do her share at the day-care center lest she be thought of as someone who refuses to do her fair share of the work.

These matters tie in with the idea of how to be a responsible member of society and the very strong constraint to act of one's own free will to benefit the public good. The importance of being cooperative, of being a good team member and working well in groups is important. Individuals should pull hard for the group because what is good for the group will eventually pay dividends for the individual. Collective action is seldom good as an end in itself, but a cooperative system is necessary to permit the individual to do things which he could not do for himself.

Usually one has a choice of how exactly to be helpful, but circumstances sometimes force the choice. When a river is overflowing its banks and threatening the community, people must respond. In rural areas, most fire protection is rendered by volunteer firemen who choose to work without pay. At the scene of an actual fire, however, it is not uncommon to see people who would not *choose* to spend time fighting fires actually doing so. In an *emergency*, one should do what one can and take pride in being able to do a lot.

Thus, Livia behaved properly in the restaurant by tendering emergency aid to Carol—quickly giving her water to drink which she had brought along as a proper preventive measure against the food on the Thruway. Her competence shows the incompetence of the restaurant staff in its worst light. They were not called upon to do anything extraordinary. Rather, Carol suggests in her telling that they were unable to do their jobs because they were much less than proper people. Mentally retarded and "crazy" people who can not do their jobs are excluded from the responsibilities of adulthood. Only someone who is not a proper person does his job inadequately. Not being able to perform one's work competently is a mark of very great shame, since one is paid to work well. One is almost stealing to take money for a job one cannot do.

4.5 "The Baddest Girl in the Neighborhood"

"The Baddest Girl in the Neighborhood" also involves bad people: the "baddest girl" whom the narrator was forced to fight, more or less against his will. The Adequate Paraphrase of the story, arrived at after long analysis, is as follows:

The narrator hit the "baddest girl in the neighborhood" because he could not tolerate being bullied for having no money.

A Story about Standing Up for Your Rights
In order to understand why this story was tellable, we need to understand what is storyworthy about a bad girl, about fighting a girl and about fighting when one would rather not do so.

Let's take these various points in order and begin by asking what a "bad girl" is and why one could build an (American) story around one. Since the second question is easier to answer than the first, we will begin with it:

A Bad Girl

A story about a bad girl is narratable because it is illustrative of a *deviation* from proper behavior and thus demonstrates the expectations about proper conduct which speaker and hearer both share. The girl in the story is bad because she extorts money and candy from other children, threatening them with violence if they do not accede to her demands. She is blackmailing them, using their fear of being beaten up as a club to get them to do what she wants.

What is wrong with blackmail and extortion is that the strong must help the weak and not exploit their relative lack of power. Reminding someone of his inferiority, let alone preying on that inferiority, makes the inferior unhappy, takes away from his sense of self-worth makes him feel himself to be less than a person since all persons are equal. Making someone feel bad is wrong because it hurts to feel badly and it is wrong to hurt other people, unless it is in their own interest. Extorting by threat of violence puts the weaker person in a box with no means of escape: his freedom of action and possibility of choice are very severely limited. Should he resist the extortion attempt, the violent repercussion will make him feel his powerlessness. Should he agree to the extortionist's demands, he is powerless by virtue of his capitulation since he would have shown himself to be too weak to stick up for himself.

Someone who refuses to resist the outrage to one's sense of worth which an extortionist's demand represents is not acting like a man. By refusing to stick up for himself, the weak person proves himself to be morally weak and therefore deserving of his fate. A morally correct individual will not give in to coercion even if the odds are heavily against him because to do so would be cowardly. What is narratable about fighting this bad girl is that the narrator is showing himself to be a proper person and not a coward.

Let us consider this question of cowardice for a bit. Rather than use a "how-to-live-your-life-book" as a source of American wisdom on this score, let us look at part of a discussion of Tonga views towards cowardice taken from an anthropological study of these people:

Tonga imagination . . . provides other interpretations . . . [of valorous deeds] . . . They find no virtue in the last ditch defense and no shame in cowardice . . . *they do not expect others to choose death as a protest against the force of an opponent or as witness to the rightness of a cause, or to court death or serious injury for reputation's sake.* (Colson in Beidelman, 1971, p. 23. emphasis added)

The last sentence gives some strong indication of an Anglo-Saxon view of cowardly behavior: giving in to odds, abandoning a worthy cause because the chance of success are slim, saving one's skin rather than face danger. Why are these wrong?

Simply put, cowardly behavior reinforces the evil forces which oppress the weak. To refuse to give way before a strong enemy assures the enemy of some pain in his victory and may act as a deterrent for further oppressors. It is morally wrong of the oppressed to allow themselves to be subjugated, to accept less than equal status. Cowardly behavior acts against the common good and against the best interests of the individual, since giving in to oppression may result in an unnecessary victory. Underlying a rejection of cowardly behavior is a notion of optimism. Things may well improve and the valorous will share in the spoils while the cowardly will have guaranteed defeat.

In this story, the narrator's decision to fight the baddest girl despite his slim chances of success signalled his understanding and participation in the norms of brave, that is, noncowardly behavior. His action was brave insofar as her strength was superior to his, and it was justified because his cause was right, or at least because her extortionist cause was wrong. Standing up for his *rights* was the action not only of a brave man, but also of a proper person. To allow himself to be oppressed would have been bad for him since he would have lived in fear, while acting courageously might well have also had good social effect, though he does not say so. By refusing to give in to her demands, the narrator made a choice to defend his freedom of action and independence of behavior.

4.6 *"The Ordeal"*[3]

"The Ordeal," the opening story of the "Kate's Triumph" sequence, is also about courage, the opposite of cowardice. Many of the themes in this story, built upon constructs which were discussed at some length in the examination of other stories.

So far , in this chapter, we have attempted to "open out" the argument, to try to explore as many non-redundant aspects of the stories as possible. However, in the closing sections, dealing with "Kate's Triumph" and "The Robbery," significant redundancies are explored. This strategy is designed, in part, to close the discussion with a demonstration of the limited set of possible story materials available within a culture. Though considerably larger than the set we have found operating within these stories, in its most essential elements, the narratable set is relatively small.

"The Ordeal": A Story of Courage

"The Ordeal" takes place in the delivery room of the hospital in which Kate gave birth to her baby. As told, it is a story of pain, courage, and "spunk." Let us begin with the Adequate Paraphrase of the story:

Despite a very long and painful childbirth, Kate asks the doctor a million questions. Although she has lost a lot of blood and is "almost dead" she still appreciates her doctor explaining unpleasant material to her in a "straightforward" way.

This paraphrase offers a considerable amount of culturally salient material suitable for exploration.

In general, "The Ordeal" is a story of courage. As such it is related to "The Baddest Girl," which is also about physical courage, although Kate triumphed over her own pain, while the narrator of the previous story dealt with a human adversary. We

---

3 Both "The Ordeal" and "The Robbery" are too long to deal with in their entireties; therefore only parts of the stories will be analyzed.

need to understand why it is worth reporting Kate's physical condition in order to understand why asking a great many questions in such a state might be dealt with in a story. We will also discuss why Kate appreciated the doctor's straightforward explanation and why that appreciation might function as one of a story's points.

While facing an enemy might be painful and difficult, calling for a certain type of courage—a courage with strong social utility—facing one's own pain, physical or mental, calls for courage of a more personal nature. Why is it courageous to face pain? Because pain hurts and it is normal not to want to feel something that hurts. Only a masochist would rather feel pain than not feel pain: however, growing and changing, both of which are necessary and beneficial experiences, involve pain and an individual who wants to grow must accept the pain involved. Therefore, pain must be borne but it must not be enjoyed.

Courageous people do not enjoy pain, but they bear it with fortitude, without making life unpleasant or difficult for other people. Thus, an understanding how much physical pain someone is in gives a measure of how courageous a person he is. Someone who goes to pieces over a splinter is a weakling; someone who cannot bear the pain of having a tooth extracted without an anaesthetic may well be acceptable; and a soldier whose leg is amputated on the battlefield while he is fully conscious and does not cry out is very courageous.

There are several issues raised by these observations. First, one can cause other people distress by making a fuss. Second, one can assess how much pain is warranted by various physical problems. Finally, one has a right to be upset by the discomfort. Why is being upset by one's pain something to need to have a right to? Because someone else's pain is painful to an observer. Therefore, someone who is in pain and shows that he is in pain himself inflicts pain. In order to inflict pain without being wrong, one must have the right to inflict it. Who can inflict pain on whom is very tightly circumscribed: in general, the strong can punish the weak with just cause—i.e. either to help the punished learn some lesson, or to protect society from wrongdoing. Someone can also inflict pain without on us if he cannot help himself from doing so.

Full adult human beings are sufficiently in control of themselves that they can prevent themselves from inflicting pain. Therefore, someone who inflicts pain without meaning to is, by definition, not acting correctly and is less than a full human being, and has forfeited his full adult status by being unable exert self-control. A child-abuser may not be legally responsible for his actions if he is judged to be sick, but neither is he a fully acceptable adult.

Someone who enjoys inflicting pain or watching others in pain is a sadist, another sort of sick, that is, wrong person. Since being in pain itself causes other people pain, there is a very strong taboo against making a fuss and causing other people pain. Even small children will often apologize for expressing their pain, crying out that they are sorry while protesting against the pain itself. Adults, too, often apologize to doctors or nurses for being overcome by pain as well as to their friends and relatives, who, being closer to them, are more vulnerable to being hurt by their distress. It is very interesting that pain and apology are so closely connected, perhaps due to the familiar and previously discussed association of pain with wrongdoing. Because pain can be mental as well as physical—seeing someone else in pain hurts the observer, or should hurt the observer since it is callous not to react to another's suffering. The pain for the observer is, of course, not physical but mental pain. Mental or emotional pain is so well established that it is possible to get a divorce on the grounds of physical or mental abuse and to recover damages through court action for mental anguish.

One suffers mental pain by being deprived of a non-physical need.

Young children need to be loved—that is, they require a certain amount of love and esteem, help and support, from the persons around them if they are to survive well physically and develop sufficient self-love, self-esteem, and self-confidence to become healthy and effective personalities. (Ellis and Harper, 1961, pp. 30-31)

A child who does not receive love, will not become a healthy adult, and health is very important. Though one may disagree on what is healthy, one cannot argue that being healthy is not important. Therefore, an argument such as the one quoted above becomes a very potent one indeed. A child deprived of love will be unable to develop "self-love, self-esteem, and self-confidence" needed for a healthy, effective, competent self. And it is of overwhelming importance to nourish the self because no one else will care for someone who does not take care of himself.

Remember after a certain time in your life *whatever* gets done is up to you. [Emphasis authors'] (Newman and Berkowitz, 1977, p. 12)

Without the satisfaction of basic physical needs, a person will die. Basic non-physical needs such as love, acceptance, comfort, companionship, caring, help in times of stress or pain which are satisfied by parents for their children must be satisfied by the adult for himself. There is no one else. We are all really alone.

An adult must face his life courageously, put up with pain in order to show that he is self-sufficient, not involve others unnecessarily in his pain. An adult knows that he is alone. Only dependent, sick, wrong people believe that other people are there to help them when they are in need. One's friends will help, of course, but only if we do not need help, but are merely in a position where being helped would be useful. Needing anything other than the self is unhealthy, and needing the self is the basic tenet of human existence. Without a competent, strong, courageous self, one has nothing, one cannot survive.

Kate's spunk, her willingness and eagerness to ask a million questions despite her pain and loss of blood was an indication of her courage and her strong and positive attitude toward life. Since life is always changing, always new, and there are always possibilities for new experiences, it is imperative that the individual not succumb to inertia and cut himself off from exciting opportunities. Kate's wants to *know* all about her world, to be in control of what was happening to her, to be able to make choices and decisions. She does not want to be a passive participant in her own life but a fully responsible adult. Her asking questions in such different circumstances in which there is no expectation of such active involvement indicates that she is the fully adult person she wants to be. The doctor's straight-forward answers to Kate's questions, which detailed the unpleasant nature of her difficulties, bore witness to her respect for Kate's praiseworthy and fully adult behavior. To deny someone knowledge of his condition is an insult showing that he is not fully adult, not fully capable of accepting reality. Kate's whole-hearted acceptance of reality as evidenced by her enthusiastic response to the doctor's comments validates both the respect of the doctor and the respect of the recipients of her story—Kate is truly worthy of respect since not only did she withstand the pain and want to know insistently and courageously, but she also responded positively to what might have been thought unpleasant news. Kate can take it. Nancy and Susan, the protagonists and co-tellers of "The Robbery" may be less able to take it or what they were forced to take may be more than a proper person can manage.

4.7 "The Robbery": A Story of Fear and Victimization

"The Robbery" is a long story with many points emphasized at different moments through the talk, including Nancy and Susan's ability to identify their assailants because of the auditory acuity of one and the visual acuity of the other. At some moments, it is a story of competence, very much like the other stories in which control over experience is a central them. However, strength and competence are only aspects of the story. If we look carefully and consider carefully all of the propositions in the storyworld and the various types of evaluation both through pseudo-conversation and other devices, we come to a much blacker picture. The explosive sound from the story recipients which greeted Nancy's remark about the gun being a foot from her head was not a sound of admiration for her courage but an expression of awe for the fear that encounter engendered.

  Let us begin this final look at the world evoked through the stories analyzed in this book with the following Adequate Paraphrase of "The Robbery":

Susan and Nancy were very frightened because they might have been killed when they were robbed at gunpoint by people who will not be convicted.

If this Paraphrase is broken down into constituent propositions, the following list results:

1. Susan and Nancy were very frightened.
2. Susan and Nancy might have been killed.
3. Susan and Nancy were robbed at gunpoint.
4. The people who robbed Susan and Nancy will not be convicted.
5. The people who robbed Susan and Nancy were very frightening.

The first point which concerns being frightened was discussed earlier in the discussion of the meaning of Proposal I of "Fainting on the Subway." The second point, however, has not been explored specifically, although many of the analyses have touched on related issues.

Why is being killed frightening?There are two closely related reasons: one because it is frightening to die and the other because it is frightening to be forced to die prematurely, violently, and with full knowledge of the impending event.

It is frightening to die because dying represents the final abdication of control. Dying is the separation from the self and the ultimate helplessness without even a consciousness to deal with the helplessness and protect the self against it. Death is the end and the end is the ultimate horror. The gun which the robbers had, could have killed Nancy and Susan. The women's terror was appropriate when they felt fear at the presence of the gun.

Being robbed is upsetting even without the threat of extermination. Being robbed deprives a person of his possessions, reduces him to penury. Adults have possessions; with possessions, with money, they can care for themselves, take care of their own needs. Reduced to dependence by being penniless is a sign of weakness, of being unable to care for yourself. The poor man is punished for his wrongdoing by being poor. Susan and Nancy lose not only their money but also their ability to manage for themselves. By being robbed, they themselves become people who are wrong. And people who are wrong ought to be punished. Their quandary is that *they* were punished and thus became wrong, while the robbers who deprived them of their goods, of their pride, will not be convicted, will not lose their freedom—a prerogative of adults—and by the logic of getting what you deserve, end up vindicated while they, the victimized, stand convicted by their own loss.

The robbers were frightening people because they did not hesitate to use violence, or threats of violence, against other people, thus putting themselves in the same group as the Nazi exterminators of "Fainting on the Subway" and the bully of "The Baddest Girl in the Neighborhood," As Nancy says, therefore, it is a frightening world:

"It's terrible to be at the mercy of such people."

With such people at liberty, the virtuous are no longer safe, the defenseless—those without guns—are no longer safe, and no longer safe, are no longer virtuous, since one must take all necessary steps to save oneself. Otherwise, one has failed and one deserves what happens next. This is familiar reasoning. It is the reasoning which reacts to tragedy with shame; it is the reasoning which condemns the victims of the Holocaust; it is the reasoning which justifies the mounting arsenals; it is the reasoning which may bring about the end of the world. It is American reasoning which leads to an un-American conclusion. The end of an American story, as Hollywood knows and everyone knows, cannot be so somber. Pessimism, the "realism" of Europe, is pretentious in America. Hopelessness is ruled out because problems call for action, call for solution. "Don't just stand there, do something." and soon it will be clear that "Every cloud has a silver lining." "There's no place to go but up," after all.

Constructing the Grammar
of American Culture

In this chapter, the recurring, important cultural constructs which have been emerging from this discussion will be arranged into a grammar which attempts to make explicit the relationships obtaining among them. Before going on to group the constructs, however, it is necessary to decide what should be considered a "construct" at all. In order to show how these culturally primitive notions were distilled from this very free-flowing, nonanalytic treatment of the stories, working though an analysis of an example sentence might well be moie elucidating than an abstract methodological description.

5.1 Abstracting Out Cultural Constructs

Beginning with sentences taken from the analysis of the stories, such as this one from the discussion of "The Ordeal" (Section 4.5):

Kate is truly worthy of respect since not only did she withstand the pain, wanted to know insistently and courageously, but she also responded positively to what might have been thought unpleasant news.

a transformation was made to re-organize the sentence syntactically into as simple a form as possible:

1. Kate should be respected because she withstood pain and wanted to "know" and responded positively to unpleasant news.

Those statements were then unpacked into simpler propositions:

2.
    a. Being respected is a good thing—people want to be respected.
    b. Some people are respected—there is some sort of important distinction being made between those who are respected and those who are not.
    c. People are respected who do certain types of things.
    d. "Withstanding pain," "wanting to know," "being courageous," and "responding positively to unpleasant news" are all examples of those things which deserve respect.

From elsewhere in the investigations (and by virtue of being a cultural initiate) I know that it is also true that:

3.
    a. "Withstanding pain" is difficult and praiseworthy;
    b. "Wanting to know" is important;
    c. "Being courageous" is difficult and praiseworthy;

Therefore:

4. People who do things which are important, difficult and praiseworthy are   worthy of respect.

Given 2a ("Being respected is a good thing—people want to be respected") the following list of culturally significant propositions can be inferred:

5.
    a. People should withstand pain;
    b. People should want to know;
    c. People should be courageous;
    d. People should be able to "take it" well;
    e. People want to be respected.

Now, given that 5a ("People should withstand pain") is not an absolute statement about the world, but is a conditional statement, it is possible to continue the unpacking process further.

Presumably, some people do withstand pain and others do not, some people should be respected and others should not be. The distinction is more intuitive, less clear, than that distinguishing between something which IS NOT, for example. People who DO what they SHOULD DO are people acting correctly, what we will call PROPER PEOPLE to distinguish them from the rest of humanity with whom they share the common features grouped under the heading PEOPLE. PROPER PEOPLE is, therefore, a special category of PEOPLE, and, also, a special category of ADULTS. PROPER PEOPLE inherit all of the features of ADULTS because they are those PEOPLE who do what ADULTS KNOW they SHOULD DO.

These sorts of distinctions among categories of PEOPLE are extremely important for the members of the group which makes them.

For example, in many aspects of the American life, it matters legally if someone is a CHILD or an ADULT. We EXPECT different behavior from people of different sorts. They have different RIGHTS and NEEDS etc. and those items, RIGHTS and NEEDS, are REAL, they matter and we can debate exactly what is a RIGHT and what is a NEED and what is, somewhat less compelling, a WANT. Should a person be hungry and steal food because he does not work and has no money, the judgment of culpability is quite different depending on what class of person he is. A CHILD need not work, indeed cannot work, and should he be hungry someone else is at fault because some ADULT or ADULTS in the aggregate (SOCIETY) did not provide him with a basic human NEED (food). Should the culprit BE an ADULT who does not work, the issue is quite a bit more complex; a number of different constructs begins to come into play. If the ADULT does not work because there is no work then he may or may not be guilty of being a very improper person (i. e. criminal). Every ADULT should be able to provide for his own NEEDS; failure to do so makes him less than a PROPER PERSON. However, if there is no work for him to do then there may be debate about his RESPONSIBILITY. Should he not work because he DOES NOT WANT to work, then he is clearly guilty because he is not DOING what an ADULT MUST DO.

Political arguments, disagreements of all sorts, struggles among the various interest groups in American Society revolve around these sorts of issues. We agree that there are NEEDS, RIGHTS, RESPONSIBILITIES, and given that "all men are created equal" and should have the RIGHT TO "equal opportunity," the question of what exactly is a RIGHT or a NEED arises constantly.

For example, is the opportunity for having sexual relations a PHYSICAL NEED or a PLEASURE? Prisoner Rights groups may argue that it is a NEED while Law and Order advocates may consider it a PLEASURE (i. e. a WANT). Being forced to concede that sex is pleasurable, a Rights Group may then insist that it is both a PLEASURE and a NEED and that, indeed, HUMAN BEINGS have a RIGHT to PLEASURE.

Not every American would agree with every one of those statements and not everyone will agree that the constructs on the List of Constructs are arranged correctly or that the lists are precisely the right set of constructs. However, this does not, in itself, diminish the validity of the lists. Most of us who consider ourselves to be American have something to say about each item on the Lists and about each statement in the previous short discussion or the extended discussion of classes of PERSON which follows the Lists themselves. Although we may not agree that "ADULTS MUST ACT in the face of DANGER," for example, some of us may see this statement as an absolute condition of ADULTHOOD and other believe it to be more accurately a SHOULD, however all of us would agree 1) some PEOPLE ARE ADULTS; 2) DOING/ACTING is something PEOPLE DO; 3) some things are DANGEROUS; 4) ADULTS MUST DO some things and 5) SHOULD DO other things. Thus these constructs have meaning, and the relations among the primitive elements which constitute them are worth thinking and talking about. We know that we are dealing with culturally salient material when we can dispute the boundary lines among categories and find it important to do so but agree that the primitive elements are real, important, and primary. Cross-culturally, the primitive elements may have similar names, but the relations among these elements might well be very very different without the common ground of agreement of members of the same culture.

Some time ago, I had a discussion with an Italian friend. We were talking about RIGHTS. He insisted that RIGHTS are given to the INDIVIDUAL by SOCIETY. SOCIETY NEEDS literate PEOPLE more than illiterate ones, for example, and therefore GRANTS the INDIVIDUAL the RIGHT to an EDUCATION.

I was somewhat dumbfounded by this argument even though I could not refute it. I certainly agree that an EDUCATED PERSON is more USEFUL to SOCIETY than one who cannot read or write. However, the argument seemed totally backwards. The INDIVIDUAL, in my AMERICAN scheme, *HAS* RIGHTS by virtue of being an INDIVIDUAL PERSON. SOCIETY consists somewhat amorphously of the government, other people, and everything importantly composed from a GROUP of PEOPLE of which the INDIVIDUAL is one. SOCIETY, such as it is, *MUST RESPECT* the RIGHTS of the INDIVIDUAL, but cannot *GRANT RIGHTS TO* the INDIVIDUAL.

The distinction is a crucial one. In one case, the Italian, SOCIETY is at the core of the WORLD and must be protected. It is also granted the role of actor much more than in the American scheme in which the INDIVIDUAL is actor at the center of the WORLD and SOCIETY is, as one American friend put it, "just a bunch of INDIVIDUALS anyway." SOCIETY is not even found on our Lists because it seemed that everything which could be said about SOCIETY was somehow reducible to the relationship of one INDIVIDUAL to OTHER INDIVIDUALS. SOCIETY need not be mentioned specifically, as long as the INDIVIDUAL and his RELATIONSHIP with OTHER PEOPLE were both included. Seemingly, and this is the claim being made here, an Italian Grammar of Cultural Constructs would be very different from the American Grammar presented here.

5.2 Structuring the Lists of Cultural Constructs

A compendium of cultural constructs could take the form of a simple list of statements which might read, for example:

1. ALL PEOPLE SHOULD BE HEALTHY
2. ALL PEOPLE DO NEED
3. ALL PEOPLE SHOULD BE HAPPY

Such a list would be convenient because each individual statement would be present in its full form, easy to read and to understand. However, a bit more structure seems necessary even for this simple three item list. Obviously, sentences (1) and (3) are more closely related to one another than they are to (2) since (1) and (3) have in common ALL PEOPLE SHOULD BE while (2) shares only ALL PEOPLE with them.

(1), (2) and (3) are all taken from this list below, in which all of the ALL PEOPLE SHOULD BE statements are grouped together, all of the ALL PEOPLE DO statements are grouped together, and so on.

(II.A.9)   ALL PEOPLE SHOULD BE HEALTHY.
              ALL PEOPLE SHOULD BE HAPPY.
              ALL PEOPLE SHOULD BE TRUSTWORTHY.
              ALL PEOPLE SHOULD BE ADULTS.
              ALL PEOPLE SHOULD WANT what PEOPLE WANT

(II.A.4)   ALL PEOPLE DO NEED.
              ALL PEOPLE DO think.
              ALL PEOPLE DO communicate, etc.

(II.A.5)   ALL PEOPLE CAN ACT one way and BE another.
              ALL PEOPLE CAN MANIPULATE OTHER PEOPLE.
              ALL PEOPLE CAN BE BAD OR GOOD.
              ALL PEOPLE CAN BE COMPETENT or INCOMPETENT.

(The numbers and letters in parenthesis (II.A.4) etc. indicate where these constructs are to be found in the Grammar in Chapter 7.)

Clearly, the redundancy in these lists is enormous. For example, (II.A.5) could be rewritten in an outline form as

ALL PEOPLE CAN
    1. ACT one way and BE another
    2. MANIPULATE OTHER PEOPLE
    3. BE
        a . BAD or GOOD
        b. COMPETENT or INCOMPETENT

In such a form, the more specific elements inherit the properties of the more general predicate. Only those elements which undergo change are mentioned explicitly. Higher level elements remain unchanged.[1] These organized lists of statements are all parts of a Psychology of HUMAN NATURE, which is one of the two highest level structures of the list, the other one being THE NATURE OF THE WORLD [an Ontology]. The other parts of HUMAN NATURE are about ADULTS and about being A PROPER PERSON [a Compendium of Virtues]. Parts of the subdivisions of the high level organization are as follows:

I. NATURE OF THE WORLD
   A. FACTS
II. HUMAN NATURE
   A. ALL PEOPLE
      1. MUST
      2. HAVE
         a. NEEDS
         b. FEELINGS
         c. INALIENABLE RIGHTS
      3. ARE
      4. DO
      5. CAN
      6. WANT TO BE
   B. ADULTS
      1. ARE
      2. MUST
         a. BE
         b. DO
         c. HAVE
      3. SHOULD NOT
      4. SHOULD
         a. DO
         b. HAVE

---

[1] This is essentially how Panini organized his grammar of Sanskrit.

> C. A PROPER PERSON
>   1. IS
>   2. DOES
>   3. HAS

In Chapter 8, many of these high level elements are drawn together into a "Story" detailing some of the types of persons existing in America. In this composite text, statements such as this appear:

CHILDREN HAVE FEELINGS, as do all PEOPLE, and if they DO NOT FEEL SAFE or FEEL HAPPY they ARE often unABLE to CONTROL their PAIN at UNSATISFIED NEEDS.

Exactly which NEEDS PEOPLE HAVE, for example are not spelled out. They are specified in the Grammar itself. In this case, the NEEDS an INDIVIDUAL HAS by virtue of BEING a PERSON can be found in Section II. (HUMAN NATURE), A. (ALL PEOPLE), 2. (HAVE), a. (NEEDS).

In order to make the Grammar—as these structured lists are called—more accessible, a List of Lists is included in Chapter 6. It contains only the higher level categories, showing their relationships to one another. The details can then be found in the Grammar itself.

In the List of Lists, words or phrases in capital letters, for example FRIENDS, occur repeatedly in the Grammar as more or less important primitive elements. Some terms such as SOCIAL NEEDS are further specified in subsidiary lists.

Words or phrases in small letters are either words used to connect the Primitives ("for," "what") or items which do not occur repeatedly. Many of the capitalized words are found as primitive elements in Chapter 8, "An American Story."

The List of Lists and the Grammar follow in the next two chapters.

6

A List of Lists of American Cultural Constructs

I. NATURE OF THE WORLD

    A. FACTS
        1. THINGS THAT EXIST
        2. THINGS THAT DO NOT EXIST
    B. THINGS THAT ARE POSSIBLE
    C. THE PHYSICAL WORLD
    D. LIFE IS
    E. REASONS why an "Organism" ACTS

II. HUMAN NATURE

    A. ALL PEOPLE
        1. MUST
            a. CHOOSE
            b. EARN RIGHTS
            c. DO (SATISFY NEEDS)
            d. HAVE
                (1) KNOWLEDGE
                (2) WORK
                (3) FRIENDS
        2. HAVE
            a. NEEDS
                (1) SOCIAL
                (2) EMOTIONAL
                (3) for SENSE OF SELF

               (4)   for FLEXIBILITY

               (5)   PHYSICAL

        b.   FEELINGS

               (1)   ARE

        c.   INALIENABLE RIGHTS

        d.   PAIN

    3.   ARE

        a.   INDIVIDUALS who

               (1)   ARE

               (2)   DO

               (3)   MAY

               (4)   MUST

               (5)   HAVE

                      (a)   "TRUE SELF"

                      (b)   SELF

               (6)   SHOULD NOT

    4.   DO

    5.   CAN

    6.   WANT TO BE

    7.   DO NOT WANT

    8.   MAY BE

        a.   HAPPY

        b.   COURAGEOUS

        c.   STRONG

        d.   RATIONAL

        e.   RIGHT/WRONG

    9.   SHOULD

B. ADULTS

    1.   ARE

    2.   MUST

        a.   BE

        b.   DO

        c.   HAVE

        d.   BE ABLE TO

        e.   KNOW

      f.   WANT

      g.   NEED

   3. SHOULD NOT

   4. SHOULD

      a.   DO

      b.   HAVE

      c.   BE

C. A PROPER PERSON

   1. IS

   2. DOES

   3. HAS

   4. DOES NOT

   5. IS ABLE TO

A Grammar of American Cultural Constructs

1. NATURE OF THE WORLD

   A. FACTS—Cultural entities or qualities whose existence is beyond dispute.
      1. THINGS THAT EXIST
         a. TRUTH
         b. CHANGE
         c. GROWTH
         d. CHOICE
         e. NEEDS
         f. PAIN
         g. RESPONSIBILITY
         h. RIGHTS
         i. GUILT
         j. HAPPINESS
         k. REALITY
         l. "REAL" WORLD
         m. FEELING
         n. "REAL FEELINGS"
         o. WHAT CAN BE KNOWN THROUGH THE SENSES
         p. UNDERSTANDING
         q. RESOURCES
         r. THE SELF
         s. THE "TRUE SELF"
         t. COURAGE
         u. STRENGTH

v. FUN

w. WORK

x. HISTORY

y. EQUALITY

z. FRIENDS

aa. RELATIONSHIPS

bb. TIME

cc. PAST/PRESENT/FUTURE

dd. LOSS

ee. GAIN

ff. MONEY

gg. EXCHANGE

hh. VALUE

ii. SOCIETY

jj. BEST INTERST

kk. KNOWING

ll. DOING

mm. EFFECTS OF ONE'S ACTIONS

nn. RIGHT/WRONG

oo. HOPE

pp. THREATS

qq. LIFE

rr. INSANITY

ss. BEING UNABLE TO STAND SOMETHING

tt. INCOMPETENCE

uu. FREEDOM

vv. PREDICITON

ww. COHERENCE

xx. HEALTH/SICKNESS

yy. FACTS

zz. WINNING/LOSING

aaa. TRUST

bbb. SAFETY

ccc. DANGER

ddd. The INDIVIDUAL

eee. PLEASURE

fff. NECESSITIES

ggg. MITIGATING CIRCUMSTANCES

hhh. FAIRNESS

iii. PROBLEMS

jjj. SOLUTIONS TO PROBLEMS

kkk. OTHER PEOPLE

lll. THINGS PEOPLE
- (1) CANNOT
    - (a) TOLERATE
    - (b) CONTROL
- (2) ARE NOT REPONSIBLE FOR

2. THINGS THAT DO NOT EXIST

a. ABSOLUTE SAFETY

b. SOMEONE ELSE TO REALLY SATISFY ALL OF ONE'S NEEDS

c. STABILITY—Total PREDICTABILITY

B. THINGS THAT ARE POSSIBLE but must be worked for

1. CHANGE for the better

2. "WINNING"

3. KNOWING the TRUTH

4. SOLVING PROBLEMS

5. "REAL" COMMUNICATION

6. CONSENSUS

7. CONTROL of

a. SELF

b. OTHERS

c. ENVIRONMENT

8. MAKING A DECISION CORRECTLY

9. HAVING A MEANINGFUL EFFECT

10. A "REAL" CHOICE

11. BEING FREE

12. SATISFYING NEEDS

13. PREDICTING FUTURE WORLD

C. THE PHYSICAL WORLD
 1. IS
     a. ALWAYS CHANGING
     b. ALWAYS THE SAME
     c. ALL THAT "REALLY" EXISTS
     d. INDIFFERENT
     e. KNOWable
     f. UNSAFE (often)
 2. CAN BE
     a. CONTROLLED (in part)
     b. CHANGED (in large part)
     c. COMPLEX
 3. IMPOSES REAL constraints

D. LIFE IS
 1. ALWAYS
     a. CHANGING
     b. THE SAME
 2. FAIR—"You get what you deserve"
 3. NOT FAIR—"You don't always get what you deserve"
 4. PRECIOUS
 5. SHORT

E. REASONS an "Organism" ACTS in order to
 1. SURVIVE
 2. SATISFY NEEDS
 3. SOLVE PROBLEMS
 4. GAIN COHERENCE

II. HUMAN NATURE

A. ALL PEOPLE
 1. MUST
     a. CHOOSE—Choice
         (1) EXISTS
         (2) IS A RESPONSIBILITY
         (3) IS INESCAPABLE

b.   EARN RIGHTS—FULFILL RESPONSIBILITIES

c.   DO (SATISFY NEEDS)

d.   HAVE in order to DO

    (1)   KNOWLEDGE which

        (a)   EXISTS

        (b)   PERMITS CONTROL over the WORLD

        (c)   ALLOWS FOR SOLVING OF
              PROBLEMS

        (d)   GIVES POWER to the possessor

        (e)   MAKES WORLD MAKE SENSE:

             -    Permits PLANNING

             -    Increases FEELING OF SAFETY

    (2)   WORK which

        (a)   EXISTS

        (b)   MUST BE DONE

        (c)   IS NOT FUN

        (d)   IS IMPORTANT

        (e)   Pays—PERMITS PERSON to buy
              (SATISFY)

             -    NEEDS

             -    PLEASURES

    (3)   FRIENDS who

        (a)   ARE

             -    USEFUL

             -    GOOD for the HEALTH

             -    PEOPLE who like each other

             -    CHOSEN

             -    SIMILAR

             -    DIFFERENT

             -    THERE when they are
                needed

             -    HONEST with each other

             -    DEMANDING

             -    SOMEONE A PERSON CAN be
                GENUINELY himself with

    (b)   DO
- take PLEASURE in their RELATIONSHIP
- RESPECT each other
- SHARE EXPERIENCES—talk to each other
- TAKE EACH OTHER'S parts in arguments
- INVEST TIME in each other

    (c)   MUST BE
- EQUALS
- HAPPY in the RELATIONSHIP

    (d)   CAN
- HURT each other for the other's BENEFIT
- SATISFY NEEDS
- overcome loneliness
- BE outgrown
- HELP
- FEEL good about SELF
- TEACH
- GUIDE
- CHALLENGE

    (e)   SHOULD BE CHANGED when no longer useful

2. HAVE

    a.   NEEDS for/which are

      (1) SOCIAL;

          (a) FRIENDS

          (b) TIES

          (c) SOMEONE TO TALK TO

      (2) EMOTIONAL;

          (a) STABILITY

          (b) SECURITY

          (c) COHERENCE (world should be predictable)

    (d)   To be LIKED

    (e)   TO FEEL

       -    HAPPY

       -    SATISFIED WITH SELF

(3)   A SENSE OF SELF

(4)   FLEXIBILITY;

    (a)   LEARNING

    (b)   GROWING

    (c)   CHANGING

(5)   PHYSICAL;

    (a)   AIR

    (b)   SPACE

    (c)   TOLERABLE TEMPERATURES

    (d)   (some) MONEY

    (e)   PRIVACY

    (f)   CLEANLINESS

    (g)   SLEEP

    (h)   WATER

    (i)   SAFETY

    (j)   FOOD;

       -    is a PLEASURE

       -    should be HEALTHY

b.   FEELINGS which

  (1)   EXIST;

    (a)   JOY

    (b)   ANGER

    (c)   PAIN

    (d)   UNHAPPINESS

    (e)   LONELINESS

    (f)   SADNESS

    (g)   FREEDOM

    (h)   HAPPINESS

    (i)   STRENGTH

    (j)   VULNERABILITY

    (k)   (There are many more FEELINGS)

(2) SHOULD BE
    (a) TRUSTED MORE THAN BEHAVIOR
    (b) ACKNOWLEDGED
(3) MAY GET "OUT OF CONTROL"
(4) INFLUENCE
    (a) BEHAVIOR
    (b) RESPONSIBILITY FOR ACTION
(5) ARE APPROPRIATE OR NOT ARE
c. INALIENABLE RIGHTS to
  (1) HAVE
    (a) PHYSICAL NEEDS SATISFIED
    (b) CHOICES
    (c) (some) POSSESSIONS
  (2) LIVE
  (3) BE
    (a) HAPPY
    (b) HEALTHY
  (4) TRUST THAT THE WORLD MAKES SENSE
d. PAIN (occasionally) which
  (1) EXISTS
  (2) HURTS
  (3) CAN BE PHYSICAL (see 10 below) or
     MENTAL (see 11 below)
  (4) CAN BE WITHSTOOD
  (5) VARIES in intensity
  (6) IS UPSETTING
  (7) MAY BE
    (a) AN EXCUSE for not fulfilling
       RESPONSIBILITY
    (b) NECESSARY for
       -   GROWTH
       -   CHANGE
    (c) the RESULT of
       -   DOING WRONG
       -   CHOOSING INCORRECTLY
  (8) CAN EXPIATE FOR WRONGDOING

      (9)   CAUSES other PEOPLE to WANT to HELP

      (10)   PHYSICAL PAIN RESULTS FROM

          (a)   DEPRIVATION OF PHYSICAL NEED

          (b)   DISEASE

          (c)   LACK OF SAFETY

      (11)   MENTAL PAIN RESULTS FROM

          (a)   DEPRIVATION
               OF EMOTIONAL NEED

3.   ARE

   a.   EQUAL in RIGHTS and RESPONSIBILITIES

   b.   ALIVE

   c.   ALONE

   d   UPSET by PAIN

   e.   VULNERABLE

   f.   MORTAL

   g.   PART OF SOCIETY

   h.   INDIVIDUALS who

      (1)   ARE

          (a)   OF PRIMARY IMPORTANCE

          (b)   ALONE in the WORLD

          (c)   most important to SELF

      (2)   DO

          (a)   CHOOSE their LIFE

          (b)   CREATE their LIFE

          (c)   CONTROL their fate

      (3)   MAY

          (a)   CHANGE the WORLD

          (b)   HAVE STRONG SELF which

               -     DOES (satisfy needs)

               -     is the only "REAL" NECESSITY

             of   ADULTS

      (4)   MUST

          (a)   Rely on SELF to DO

(5) HAVE
    (a) "TRUE SELF" which
        - EXISTS (in an EMOTIONAL WORLD)
        - FEELS
        - EXPERIENCES
        - REACTS TO STIMULI
        - SURFACES in some TIMES OF STRESS
        - CAN BE KNOWN
        - IS who a PERSON REALLY IS
    (b) SELF which
        - CHANGES as a RESULT of
        - - CHOICES
        - - ACTIONS
        - - EXPERIENCE (LEARNING)
        - - TIME
        - EXISTS in the PHYSICAL and SOCIAL WORLD
        - IS the "DOER" which the WORLD assumes
        - "IS" the PERSON
    (c) INALIENABLE RIGHTS
    (d) NEEDS
    (e) PERSONAL history
    (f) FUTURE
    (g) (some) PERSONAL POWER
(6) SHOULD NOT
    (a) HURT PEOPLE
    (b) Inhibit FREEDOM or CHOICE of OTHERS (except FAMILY)
    (c) Give in

4. DO
   a. NEED
   b. think

  c. communicate

  d eat

  e. breathe

  f. FEEL

  g. eliminate

  h. WANT

  i. react

  j. CHANGE*

  k. CHOOSE*

  l. KNOW*

  m. DO (SATISFY NEEDS)*

  n. PLAN*

  o. PREDICT*[1]

5. CAN

  a. ACT one way and BE another

  b. MANIPULATE OTHER PEOPLE

  c. BE

   (1) BAD or GOOD

   (2) COMPETENT or INCOMPETENT

   (3) COURAGEOUS or COWARDLY

   (4) FOOLED

    etc.

  d. KNOW THE TRUTH

6. WANT TO BE

  a. SECURE

  b. ADULTS

  c. NORMAL

  d. HAPPY

  e. HEALTHY

  f. INDEPENDENT

  g. FREE

  h. Not tied down

---

[1] (*) Classes of persons differ on these qualities (See "List of Lists").

7. DO NOT WANT
    a. UNHAPPINESS
    b. UNPLEASANTNESS
    c. PAIN
8. MAY BE
    a. HAPPY;
        (1) NORMAL STATE OF PEOPLE
        (2) signals NEEDS are SATISFIED
    b. COURAGEOUS;
        (1) CAN withstand PAIN
        (2) WANTS to KNOW (bad news)
        (3) resists oppression
    c. STRONG;
        (1) HELP weak
        (2) CAN SATISFY NEEDS
        (3) not very VULNERABLE
    d. RATIONAL;
        (1) USES MIND to SOLVE PROBLEMS
        (2) CAN
            (a) UNDERSTAND
            (b) CONTROL FEELINGS
            (c) MAKE DECISIONS
            (d) PLAN
            (e) CHOOSE
    e. RIGHT;
        (1) KNOW the TRUTH
        (2) BEHAVE CORRECTLY
9. SHOULD
    a. BE
        (1) HEALTHY
        (2) HAPPY
        (3) TRUSTWORTHY
        (4) ADULTS
    b. WANT
        (1) what PEOPLE WANT

B. ADULTS
    1. ARE PEOPLE who
        a. SATISFY NEEDS for themSELVES
        b. CAN DO what they SHOULD and
            MUST DO to SURVIVE
        c. WORK
        d. KNOW what they MUST KNOW in order to
            DO
    2. MUST
        a. BE
            (1) RESPONSIBLE for SELF
            (2) CARING which makes them FEEL
                (a) GOOD
                (b) HELPFUL
                (c) STRONG
                (d) SAFE
        b. DO
            (1) Protect themSELVES
            (2) SATISFY (own) NEEDS
            (3) CHOOSE
            (4) DECIDE
            (5) Distinguish between REALITY and
                ILLUSION
            (6) ACT
                (a) as if ALONE
                (b) in the face of DANGER
            (7) WORK
            (8) SOLVE PROBLEMS
            (9) PREDICT
            (10) PLAN
        c. HAVE
            (1) FUTURE (hope)
            (2) SENSE OF SELF
        d. BE ABLE to
            (1) SOLVE PROBLEMS
            (2) CHOOSE PROPERLY

        (3)   ACT EFFECTIVELY on CHOICES

        (4)   CHANGE

        (5)   WITHSTAND what is BEARABLE

        (6)   MANAGE THEIR LIVES

        (7)   SURVIVE

        (8)   KNOW

   e.   KNOW

        (1)   what

               (a)   EXISTS

               (b)   DOES NOT EXIST

               (c)   IS POSSIBLE

               (d)   IS a PROBLEM

               (e)   IS in their BEST INTEREST

               (f)   are PROPER GROUNDS for a DECISION

               (g) . CAN

                     -     BE TOLERATED

                     -     BE DONE

                     -     NOT BE DONE

        (2)   about HUMAN NATURE

        (3)   how

               (a)   the WORLD IS

               (b)   to PROTECT themSELVES

               (c)   to SOLVE PROBLEMS

               (d)   to SATISFY NEEDS

               (e)   to DISTINGUISH between

                     -     TRUTH and FALSEHOOD

                     -     REALITY and ILLUSION

                     -     NEEDS and WANTS

                     -     that things ARE NOT what they SEEM

        (4)   whom to TRUST

        (5)   Whether things ARE:

               (a)   ECONOMICALLY ADVANTAGEOUS

- (b) EMOTIONALLY
  ADVANTAGEOUS;
  (make them FEEL
  - HAPPY
  - GOOD
  - STRONG
  - SAFE)
- (c) HEALTHY
- (d) IN OTHER PEOPLE'S BEST
  INTEREST
- f. WANT TO
  - (1) BE
    - (a) HAPPY
    - (b) RESPECTED
    - (c) SAFE
    - (d) HEALTHY
    - (e) LOVED
    - (f) LIKED
  - (2) HAVE PLEASURES
- g. NEED in order to be PROPER PERSONS
  - (1) TO
    - (a) KNOW
    - (b) BE ABLE TO DO
    - (c) DO
    - (d) HAVE CHOICES
  - (2) THE WORLD TO BE COHERENT
  - (3) ONLY THEMSELVES
3. SHOULD NOT
   - a. NEED OTHER PEOPLE
   - b. dwell on the past
   - c. make a fuss
   - d. leave loose ends
   - e. TAKE RESPONSIBILITY for
     PEOPLE who SHOULD
     SATISFY OWN NEEDS

4. SHOULD
   a. DO
      (1) ACT in own BEST INTEREST
      (2) ACT rather than not ACT
      (3) DECIDE PROPERLY (in own
          BEST INTEREST)
      (4) CHOOSE CORRECTLY
          for SELF
          to BE, DO, ACT like
          PROPER PERSON
      (5) MAKE FRIENDS
      (6) TRUST themSELVES
      (7) LOVE themSELVES
      (8) LIKE
          (a) themSELVES
          (b) OTHER PEOPLE
      (9) ACCEPT REALITY
      (10) CHANGE
      (11) HELP others (SATISFY
           NEEDS)
      (12) LET GO of what is not good for
           SELF
   b. HAVE
      (1) FRIENDS
      (2) RELATIONSHIPS
      (3) FUN
      (4) JOB
      (5) MONEY
   c. BE
      (1) RATIONAL
      (2) STRONG
      (3) INDEPENDENT (SATISFY own
          NEEDS)
      (4) HAPPY
      (5) COURAGEOUS

    (6)   RESPONSIBLE for
- (a)   OTHERS
- (b)   ACTIONS

    (7)   REALISTIC

    (8)   FREE

    (9)   dependable

   (10) flexible

   (11) effective

   (12) co-operative

   (13) COMPETENT (DO things well)

   (14) RATIONAL

   (15) FRIENDLY

   (16) HELPFUL

   (17) TRUSTWORTHY (WILL BE
and ACT like ADULTS ARE
and ACT)

   (18) focused on the FUTURE

C. A PROPER PERSON

   1.   IS WHAT ADULT IS and SHOULD BE

   2.   DOES WHAT ADULT DOES and CAN DO

   3.   HAS WHAT ADULT NEEDS and WANTS

   4.   DOES NOT SUFFER

   5.   IS ABLE TO
- a.   HELP OTHERS
- b.   DECIDE for OTHERS (who CANNOT DECIDE)

8

An American Story

ADULTS are INDIVIDUAL PEOPLE WHO KNOW HOW to DO what they MUST DO; CAN DO what they MUST DO; and DO it.[1] They UNDERSTAND that "There are two profound choices in life: to accept things as they exist or to accept the responsibility for changing them" (Koberg and Bagnall, 1976: 41). They HAVE the CHOICE, they HAVE the KNOWLEDGE, and they CHANGE and DO to SATISFY their NEEDS. They HAVE the RESPONSIBILITY for DOing and the RIGHT to CHOOSE what and how they should live their lives, manage their affairs, and SATISFY their NEEDS.

---

[1] In this text, as in the Lists, some words are in upper case and others in lower case. NEEDS, for example, is capitalized, while "they," "try," "instead of," "ice cream," and "mental hospital" are in small letters. The capitalized words are almost all words which appear importantly on the Lists: the uncapitalized words are of three types: (1) "connecting" words: prepositions, pronouns, conjunctions, etc. These grammatical words communicate a set of possible relationships which may well be culturally determined since they express what is, and how what is interacts with other things which also are; (2) words such as "small," "return," or "promise" which do not add very much to the discussion but help clarify a point which is being made; or (3) words such as "ice cream" or "mental hospital" which conjure up a whole world. The associations and richness of these words lend some power to our description. There are some words, "upset" is one, which felt clearly like a #2 uncapitalized word as we began our Story and then was so important to the discussion that it "grew" into a capitalized primitive.

As should be clear to all readers of this book, "An American Story" is not really a story at all since it lacks both Events and Evaluation. Rather, the Story is a grammar of possible stories. Each sentence should be read as a compressed form of a myriad of "real" stories of the sort looked at earlier and the whole text composed of these sentences results in this most general level of Story: the generic American Story.

Their NEEDS SATISFIED, they FEEL GOOD about themselves and HAVE EARNED the RIGHT to PLEASURE and HAPPINESS.

ADULTS KNOW what they SHOULD BE, what they SHOULD DO, what they SHOULD HAVE. They KNOW what is "worth bothering with." They live in the PRESENT but DECIDE what is IN THEIR BEST INTEREST for the FUTURE. They KNOW HOW THE WORLD IS, WHAT is POSSIBLE, and they USE PAST EXPERIENCE (what WAS in the PAST) to help them PLAN what to DO in the FUTURE. They KNOW that the WORLD is NOT PREDICTABLE, that they are not ABSOLUTELY SAFE because they DO NOT KNOW what will happen in the FUTURE, and NOT to KNOW is very UNSAFE. When a PERSON DOES NOT KNOW, the WORLD BECOMES INCOHERENT and the INDIVIDUAL might not BE ABLE TO STAND it and DIE (HAVE NO FUTURE) or GO CRAZY—become one who DOES NOT KNOW, CAN NOT DO and is less than an ADULT.

An ADULT MUST KNOW and MUST BE ABLE to TAKE IT, to WITHSTAND PAIN, to KNOW that he HAS a FUTURE and that the FUTURE is BETTER THAN THE PAST. KNOWing about the WORLD allows the PERSON to PLAN and if he PLANS CORRECTLY (CHOOSES what to DO REALISTICALLY), he will HAVE what he WANTS and BE ABLE to SATISFY his own NEEDS. If he does not PLAN CORRECTLY, UNDERSTAND what an ADULT MUST, then he will NOT HAVE what he WANTS and may not BE ABLE to SATISFY his own NEEDS. Therefore, NOT HAVING is proof of the FACT of NOT BEING an ADULT since an ADULT HAS what he NEEDS and CAN DO what he MUST DO in order to SATISFY those NEEDS.

EVERY INDIVIDUAL PERSON WANTS to be an ADULT, TO BE INDEPENDENT, to NEED only himSELF to SATISFY his NEEDS. The TRUTH of the WORLD is that each INDIVIDUAL IS ALONE and MUST SATISFY his own NEEDS because he CAN NOT DEPEND on anOTHER PERSON to SATISFY his NEEDS in all circumstances. An INDIVIDUAL CAN HOPE that anOTHER will ALWAYS HELP, but it IS NOT TRUE that this is the case. In order to BE SAFE, to KNOW that NEEDS will be SATISFIED, EVERY

PERSON WANTS to NEED only himSELF, because EVERY INDIVIDUAL HAS A SELF, just as he HAS a BODY and IS ALIVE. He HAS it and he HAS a FUTURE until he DIES when he no longer HAS NEEDS—for AIR, WATER, SLEEP, FOOD—or WANTS, no longer EATS, BREATHES, SLEEPS, DRINKS, ELIMINATES, or LIVES. If his SELF CAN SATISFY his NEEDS he is SAFE because he WILL HAVE a SELF until he HAS NO MORE NEEDS.

As long as he LIVES, the INDIVIDUAL MUST SOLVE PROBLEMS. THINKING, SPEAKING, ACTING, PLANNING— the INDIVIDUAL USES what he KNOWS to SATISFY his own NEEDS and the NEEDS and WANTS of OTHERS, FAMILY and FRIENDS. When there is DANGER, the ADULT ACTS to PROTECT himSELF to avoid PAIN and SUFFERING. If anOTHER PERSON SUFFERS PAIN, the ADULT MUST HELP the OTHER FEEL BETTER because PAIN and UNHAPPINESS are PROBLEMS which MUST BE SOLVED. SOLVING PROBLEMS, SATISFYING NEEDS, and OBTAINING WANTS ARE the activities of an ADULT.

PEOPLE who DO NOT KNOW and CAN NOT KNOW are not ADULTS, therefore, a PROBLEM without a SOLUTION which the INDIVIDUAL CAN DISCOVER makes him LESS, something other, than a full PERSON. It IS THREATENING to an INDIVIDUAL to find a PROBLEM which he CAN NOT SOLVE, a PERSON who CAN NOT BE HELPED or MADE HAPPY, because such a situation makes the INDIVIDUAL UNDERSTAND that HE CAN NOT DO, CAN NOT KNOW and therefore is NOT SAFE. If he CAN NOT DO what an ADULT MUST DO then he CAN NOT TRUST himSELF to TAKE CARE of his own NEEDS and he IS, indeed, ALONE, HELPLESS, and VULNERABLE like a CHILD and unlike an ADULT.

CHILDREN CAN NOT DO, DO NOT KNOW. They LEARN and CHANGE and BECOME ADULTS through TIME. As long as they are small, however, they HAVE SPECIAL NEEDS. They MUST BE CARED FOR, HELPED, LOVED, and HAVE their NEEDS SATISFIED by OTHERS who LOVE them. CHILDREN HAVE a FUTURE. They HAVE the capacity to BECOME ADULTS and MUST be TAUGHT by ADULTS what the WORLD is like.

CHILDREN DO NOT KNOW and therefore CAN NOT CHOOSE how to LIVE LIFE. It is important that CHILDREN HAVE their HUMAN NEEDS and SPECIAL NEEDS satisfied because they are CHANGING as the RESULT of their EXPERIENCES of the WORLD and of OTHER PEOPLE. PEOPLE MUST HAVE a HAPPY PAST in order to TRUST the WORLD enough to BECOME PROPER PEOPLE and DO what they SHOULD DO. CHILDREN HAVE a developing SELF with its own DEVELOPING SELF INTEREST. If a CHILD IS to UNDERSTAND that HE SHOULD BE GOOD and LIVE HAPPILY with OTHER PEOPLE, he MUST UNDERSTAND that it IS in his BEST INTEREST to DO SO. The best way to show a CHILD that his BEST INTEREST lies in WORKING to SATISFY his OWN NEEDS is for the CHILD to have a CHILDHOOD which is PLEASANT enough so that he BELIEVES the WORLD to BE COHERENT and that he CAN PLAN and PREDICT and ACT to GET what HE WANTS. If a CHILD'S NEEDS went UNSATISFIED, he MIGHT LEARN that the WORLD WAS NOT a SAFE PLACE or a PREDICTABLE one and therefore he SHOULD either DO NOTHING (to PROTECT himSELF) or ACT WRONGLY (in order to GET what he NEEDed and WANTed in any way that WAS POSSIBLE.)

CHILDREN HAVE FEELINGS, as do all PEOPLE, and if they DO NOT FEEL SAFE or FEEL HAPPY they ARE often unABLE to CONTROL their PAIN at UNSATISFIED NEEDS. They may be FRIGHTENED, for example, at something which an ADULT would KNOW would not HURT them. CHILDREN are LEARNING how to PREDICT, how to PLAN, how to CONTROL their environment, their FEELINGS, and ultimately themSELVES.

CHILDREN MUST be TAKEN CARE OF, but they are not FRIGHTENING or UPSETTING to OTHER PEOPLE. Although they ARE NOT TRUSTWORTHY because they ARE NOT ABLE to CONTROL their EMOTIONS and UNDERSTAND the meaning of their ACTIONS, CHILDREN are small enough physically NOT to THREATEN OTHER PEOPLE'S HEALTH—they are not STRONG enough to HURT someone else. Since they HAVE a FUTURE, even more than a PRESENT or a PAST, they MAKE OTHER PEOPLE

HAPPY. They will GROW and BECOME ADULTS. It is not their role to be DEPENDENT and "a burden" to OTHERS until they DIE.

CHILDREN HAVE NEEDS and PROBLEMS, but an ADULT CAN HELP a CHILD and assure him that the PAIN WILL NOT LAST FOREVER and that in the FUTURE he will be HAPPY and FREE of PAIN. HELPING a CHILD is USEFUL—IS NOT "wasted effort." CHILDREN WILL BE ABLE to SATISFY their OWN NEEDS someday and they PAY for their PRESENT HELPLESSNESS with the promise of FUTURE ADULTHOOD.

CHILDREN ARE NOT ADULTS, but unlike ALL OTHER PEOPLE who DO NOT BEHAVE like ADULTS, they bring JOY to OTHER PEOPLE and represent the FUTURE. Therefore they ARE LOVED and CARED FOR while the SICK, the MORIBUND, and the RETARDED are alternatively PITIED and DESPISED; the CRAZY are PITIED and FEARED; and the POOR and the CRIMINAL are FEARED and HATED and sometimes PITIED. EACH INDIVIDUAL HAS NEEDS and HAS A RIGHT for those NEEDS to be SATISFIED. All of those PEOPLE MUST BE TAKEN CARE OF, but very few INDIVIDUALS of those groups of PEOPLE WILL ever BECOME an ADULT, LIVE PROPERLY, HAVE A FUTURE, and stop MAKING OTHER PEOPLE UNHAPPY.

The SICK may BECOME WELL. In that case, they return to their own LIVES and begin once again to SATISFY their own NEEDS. They HAVE a FUTURE and therefore can be TRUSTED to BEHAVE CORRECTLY since it is NOT in the BEST INTEREST of the INDIVIDUAL to DO anything which would MAKE him LESS HAPPY or SAFE in the FUTURE. The MORIBUND are LESS TRUSTWORTHY. They HAVE NOTHING TO LOSE. Lacking a FUTURE, they lack a BEST INTEREST and also any reason to PLAN out their ACTIONS to MAKE themselves HAPPY. They ARE DYING. They HAVE no reason to BE HAPPY. They MAKE the LIVING uncomfortable since it is PAINFUL to watch someone in TROUBLE and BE UNABLE to HELP. HELPLESSNESS in the face of a PROBLEM renders the would be HELPER HELPLESS, thus reducing him from an ADULT to a CHILD. The SICK and the

MORIBUND DESERVE some of their PAIN because they make OTHER PEOPLE SUFFER through BEING UNABLE to HELP.

CAUSING PAIN is WRONG and WRONGDOING SHOULD BE PUNISHED by PAIN. PAIN is also cleansing: it relieves the GUILT of WRONGDOING. Since the SICK PAID for their WRONGDOING by SUFFERING while they were ILL, the "score is even" and without onus they re-enter their LIVES HEALTHY and ABLE to SATISFY their OWN NEEDS. The MORIBUND DIE, of course, and their score is settled, too. They SUFFERED and MADE OTHERS SUFFER, but they "paid their debts" by dying and can BE thought of by the LIVING in terms of their LIFE as an ADULT before becoming MORIBUND and their BEHAVIOR during the time when it was clear that they HAD NO FUTURE. Since DYING is INTOLERABLE, someone who managed to STAND what CAN NOT BE STOOD and BE COURAGEOUS in the face of terrible PAIN and LOSS, may be closer in his DEATH to being a PROPER PERSON than he ever was in LIFE.

The SICK and the MORIBUND are ADULTS manqué: they KNOW what ADULTS NEED to KNOW but they CAN NOT DO. The RETARDED DO NOT KNOW and CAN NOT DO. They are CHILDREN without a FUTURE: CHILDREN manqué. As CHILDREN they DESERVE to HAVE their NEEDS TAKEN CARE OF including the SPECIAL NEEDS of CHILDHOOD: LOVE, FUN, TO BE TAUGHT. But because they are LESS than CHILDREN, their NEEDS ARE TAKEN CARE OF at a lower level. They NEED FUN, for example, but not every day; they SHOULD HAVE SPECIAL FOODS, ice cream, perhaps, but only occasionally. Because they will NEVER BE ABLE to REPAY what they ARE GIVEN, they ARE GIVEN less—only enough to SATISFY the NEED for it HAVING BEEN GIVEN, but not so much that OTHERS with MORE FUTURE will be deprived. The RETARDED in many hospitals are ranked according to how well they CAN THINK, how close to BEING an ADULT they can possibly BECOME. Those with the most capacity for KNOWING HAVE MORE NEEDS because they KNOW about their NEEDS and ARE MORE UPSET by those NEEDS BEING UNSATISFIED. In mental hospitals for the CRAZY there is the same system of ranking by distance from the ADULT. The CRAZY MAY or MAY NOT KNOW, MAY or MAY NOT BE ABLE TO DO. They ARE CONFUSED and they ARE CONFUSING. They ARE CONFUSING because they ARE CONFUSED. Their WORLD is NOT COHERENT; it MAKES NO SENSE and PEOPLE CAN NOT TOLERATE the WORLD BEING INCOHERENT. They HAVE NO CHOICE in an INCOHERENT WORLD but to GO CRAZY because they are UNABLE to PLAN or PREDICT, to FEEL SAFE or SECURE, which ARE HUMAN NEEDS. Therefore, the CRAZY PERSON HAS NO CHOICE but to remain CRAZY—NOT TO CHANGE. Someone who DOES NOT CHANGE to HELP STOP his own PAIN is CONFUSING because PEOPLE SHOULD DO that and SHOULD WANT to STOP their PAIN but CRAZY PEOPLE MAY KNOW what PEOPLE WANT and MAY WANT what PEOPLE WANT but because they KNOW that the WORLD is INCOHERENT they CAN NOT ACT to CHANGE. Since they CAN NOT ACT TO CHANGE, they have no CHOICE but to remain CRAZY and therefore they HAVE NO FUTURE, they CAN NEVER CHANGE.

Sometimes it MAY SEEM as if a CRAZY PERSON has CHANGED and BECOME an UNCRAZY, NORMAL, ADULT. But that IS an ILLUSION because REALLY in their TRUE SELVES they ARE PEOPLE who KNOW differently from OTHER PEOPLE and CAN NOT BE TRUSTED. PEOPLE DO NOT KNOW what a CRAZY PERSON thinks is in his BEST INTEREST. Someone who is so CONFUSED may THINK the WORLD is INCOHERENT and NOT BEING ABLE TO STAND IT MAY DECIDE his BEST INTEREST is different from what OTHER PEOPLE KNOW their BEST INTEREST to BE. Therefore, a CRAZY PERSON MAY BE UNPREDICTABLE and MAKE OTHERS FEEL UNSAFE because they WILL NOT KNOW what to EXPECT and PEOPLE NEED TO KNOW what to EXPECT if they ARE to FEEL SAFE. CRAZY PEOPLE are DIFFERENT PEOPLE, CONFUSING PEOPLE. ARE they ADULTS? No. ARE they CHILDREN? No. They KNOW and they CAN DO. They are DIFFERENT because they are CONFUSED and they ARE CONFUSING because they ARE DIFFERENT. But they ARE in PAIN and they CAUSE OTHER PEOPLE PAIN by their PAIN and their CONFUSION. Therefore, their SUFFERING is DESERVED. OTHER PEOPLE may PITY them but also DESPISE them for BEING WRONG, KNOWING something which is not TRUE, KNOWing an ILLUSION to BE REAL. CRAZY PEOPLE KNOW that PEOPLE NEED TIES, FRIENDS, FAMILY, and a place in a COMMUNITY. They KNOW, too, that they ARE NOT TRUSTED and DO NOT HAVE those TIES because they ARE DIFFERENT from OTHER PEOPLE. They KNOW their NEEDS ARE NOT BEING SATISFIED and they FEEL the PAIN of that deprivation. They KNOW they ARE ALONE both as EVERY INDIVIDUAL IS ALONE and even more ALONE because they DO NOT HAVE what OTHER PEOPLE HAVE to HELP them FEEL LESS ALONE even if they ARE ALONE. The CRAZY are CONFUSING because their PAIN is a PROBLEM which they CAN NOT SOLVE and which no OTHER PERSON CAN SOLVE either. Their PAIN is almost a CHOICE because they SEEM not to WANT to KNOW or ACCEPT what OTHER PEOPLE KNOW:

There are THINGS which NO ONE CAN STAND and, yet, NOT STANDING SOMETHING which NO ONE CAN STAND IS WRONG because probably the INDIVIDUAL COULD HAVE CHOSEN to STAND IT. However, if a PERSON DID NOT STAND SOMETHING and WAS in PAIN from it, and if the PERSON was a PROPER PERSON otherwise and KNEW himSELF to BE WRONG, SICK AND KNOWing things which ARE NOT REAL, then perhaps that PERSON WAS only a SICK ADULT and NOT a CRAZY PERSON and CAN BE restored to BEING an ADULT.

CRAZY PEOPLE ARE NOT RESPONSIBLE for their ACTIONS, unlike ADULTS, because they DO NOT KNOW that they ARE DOING WRONG. They may THINK (WRONGLY) that they are SATISFYING A NEED by DOING something WRONG, something which CAUSES PAIN or LOSS to OTHER PEOPLE. CRIMINALS ARE ADULTS. They ARE WRONG ADULTS and they ARE RESPONSIBLE for their ACTIONS. CRIMINALS ARE ADULTS who KNOW what ADULTS KNOW, CAN DO what ADULTS CAN DO and yet CHOOSE to DO as ADULTS KNOW they SHOULD NOT DO.

ADULTS KNOW that they MUST NOT KILL, or TAKE what someone else OWNS, or cause PAIN to ANY OTHER PERSON except in the BEST INTEREST of that PERSON. CRIMINALS KNOW all that and yet they CHOOSE to DO WRONG. They MUST BE PUNISHED. Because they CHOOSE WRONGLY, they MUST BE DEPRIVED of CHOICE: because they are ADULTS who CHOOSE NOT TO ACT RESPONSIBLY, like ADULTS—they MUST BE TREATED LIKE CHILDREN who NEED TO BE PUNISHED "for their own good," deprived of FREEDOM, of PLEASURE, of CONTROL OVER THEIR OWN LIVES. Unlike CHILDREN, they ARE NOT LOVED or considered to HAVE SPECIAL NEEDS. They ARE ADULTS and their NEEDS are the NEEDS of an ADULT, not the NEEDS of a CHILD that are only WANTS of an ADULT. Only the PHYSICAL NEEDS of criminals MUST BE SATISFIED: to EAT, to DRINK, to BE CLEAN; SOCIAL and SPIRITUAL NEEDS are left UNSATISFIED. The PAIN of UNSATISFIED NEEDS and the possibility of a FUTURE of UNSATISFIED NEEDS PAY BACK the WRONGNESS of the CRIMINAL ACT and, at the same time, TEACH the CRIMINAL that he MUST CHOOSE CORRECTLY when he HAS DECISIONS to MAKE in the FUTURE. DEPRIVING the CRIMINAL of a part of his FUTURE, of CONTROL over a part of his LIFE, is one part of the PAIN of imprisonment. He MUST PAY BACK his "debt to society" with HIS TIME, his FUTURE, his LIFE.

CRIMINALS MUST 'LEARN that WORK, which is UNPLEASANT and TIME CONSUMING for EVERYONE, MUST NOT BE AVOIDED. "Getting something for nothing" IS IMPOSSIBLE since, if NO ONE WORKED—and NO ONE WANTS to WORK—NO ONE's NEEDS WOULD BE SATISFIED. WORK is NECESSARY both for the INDIVIDUAL to SATISFY his NEEDS and for SOCIETY, the GROUP of ALL INDIVIDUALS, to SATISFY its NEEDS. NOT WORKing HURTS EVERYONE because ALL MUST WORK if LIFE IS to CONTINUE. CRIMINALS ARE, therefore, GUILTY of NOT WORKing as well as of the crime which they committed. The POOR ARE GUILTY only of NOT WORKing— of HAVING NEEDS and insufficient MEANS to SATISFY them.

The POOR KNOW that WORK is NECESSARY. They ARE POOR BECAUSE THEY ARE NOT WORKing, NOT WORKing enough, or NOT ABLE to WORK, depending on the circumstances. They KNOW that ADULTS WORK and often they MAY WANT to WORK but they ARE UNABLE to SATISFY their NEED to HAVE WORK in order to MAKE ENOUGH MONEY to SATISFY their OTHER NEEDS. Since ADULTS HAVE (some) MONEY, enough for their NEEDS, and DO WORK, the POOR ARE NOT ADULTS. If they DO WORK, they DO NOT WORK well because if they WORKED well they would be paid enough to SATISFY their NEEDS. This is only FAIR, only RATIONAL. Since they DO NOT HAVE they MUST NOT WANT or are UNABLE to WORK; in either case, the POOR ARE PEOPLE manqué—they DO NOT HAVE what they NEED and CAN NOT DO what they MUST DO in order to SATISFY them.

The POOR may BE GOOD—they MAY WANT to WORK and to DO what PEOPLE SHOULD DO in order to BE what PEOPLE SHOULD BE, but they CAN NOT and their NEEDS MUST BE TAKEN CARE OF by OTHER PEOPLE since it IS WRONG to allow any PERSON to STARVE or DIE of the COLD. They CAN NOT PAY in MONEY and, unlike the CRIMINAL, they HAVE NOT CHOSEN to ACT INCORRECTLY, so they CAN NOT BE DENIED their FREEDOM of MOVEMENT and DECISION. But they ARE WRONG because they ARE NOT ADULTS who PROVIDE for themSELVES. They ARE also UNTRUSTWORTHY since their LIVES MAY BE so UNHAPPY because of what they DO NOT HAVE and therefore CAN NOT DO that they WILL DO something which is not ordinarily in the BEST INTEREST of the INDIVIDUALS in SOCIETY who DO HAVE. They MAY LET their FEELINGS GET OUT OF CONTROL and become CRAZY or CRIMINAL—reacting to the UNBEARABLE by MAKING the WORLD UNSAFE for OTHERS. If they "have nothing to lose," they may well try to TAKE what IS not theirs instead of WORKING to BUY what they WANT like ADULTS and especially PROPER PEOPLE ARE ABLE to DO.

PROPER PEOPLE ARE those who DO what ADULTS SHOULD DO; who ARE what ADULTS should BE and who HAVE what ADULTS SHOULD HAVE. Since PEOPLE CAN NOT KNOW what OTHER PEOPLE "TRULY ARE" or exactly what they "ACTUALLY DO," they assume AN INDIVIDUAL is a PROPER PERSON if he HAS what PEOPLE WANT TO HAVE: MONEY, FAMILY, FRIENDS, a good JOB, POWER, RESPECT. Someone who HAS all that he NEEDS and WANTS IS TRUSTWORTHY because he KNOWS HOW to SATISFY his NEEDS and his KNOWing is PROVED by his NEEDS being SATISFIED. Since he is NOT a CRIMINAL, he MUST KNOW better than OTHER PEOPLE because he WANTS and CAN GET what he WANTS and they CAN NOT. He has no NEED or DESIRE to MAKE DECISIONS other than those which have ENABLED him to GET what he HAS, and since he IS who he IS and HAS what he HAS, he MUST BE someone who CAN CONTROL the WORLD sufficiently to BE HAPPY and HAVE POWER. PROPER PEOPLE ARE SAFE from NEEDS which ARE NOT SATISFIED and therefore they MAKE OTHER PEOPLE SAFE because they DO not NEED to ACT UNPREDICTABLY or INCOHERENTLY. They KNOW HOW to DECIDE and how to CHOOSE and therefore they HAVE the RIGHT to DECIDE and CHOOSE for OTHERS who CAN NOT CHOOSE, because they DO NOT KNOW or CAN NOT DO because they ARE NOT ABLE to.

PROPER PEOPLE ARE IMPARTIAL. Their NEEDS ARE SATISFIED so they NEED NOT CHOOSE "in their OWN BEST INTEREST." Their "BEST INTEREST" is BEST MET by WHAT IS and what WILL BE without CHANGE. They CAN DECIDE "on the merits" of the situation without NEEDING to "get something for themSELVES." They HAVE POWER OVER OTHER PEOPLE because they HAVE what they NEED and therefore do not NEED to USE that POWER to SATISFY their OWN NEEDS.

All People ARE EQUAL to ALL OTHER PEOPLE insofar as they ARE PROPER PEOPLE. ANY INDIVIDUAL who IS ABLE to KNOW and ABLE to DO CAN BE a PROPER PERSON. He MUST only DO what he SHOULD DO in order to KNOW what he MUST KNOW in order to DO what he MUST DO in order to HAVE what he MUST HAVE in order to BE what he SHOULD BE, what EVERY ADULT CAN BE.

We hold these Truths to be self-evident, that all Men are created Equal, that they are endowed by their Creator with certain inalienable Rights . . . among these are Life, Liberty and the Pursuit of Happiness . . . (*The Declaration of Independence of the United States of America:* July 4, 1776)

Conclusion

". . . all Men are created Equal . . . "

The Story of America is, very largely, a prolonged, complex, and sometimes tragic exegesis of those few lines from *The Declaration of Independence.* "All men are created Equal." Yes, all MEN are EQUAL. But who *exactly* are MEN? And the others, those PEOPLE who ARE NOT MEN, what RIGHTS, what LIBERTY, what FUTURE have those who ARE NOT quite ADULTS?

Over the past two hundred years, more PEOPLE, more KINDS of PEOPLE have insisted that they ARE EQUAL and "entitled to certain inalienable RIGHTS." Black PEOPLE, women, American Indians, Poor PEOPLE, gay PEOPLE and now the OLD, the HANDICAPPED and the MORIBUND DEMAND the RIGHT to DECIDE and to DO because they ARE ABLE to KNOW, ABLE to DECIDE. CRIMINALS and the INSANE are INSISTING on the RIGHT to be considered CHANGED and HEALTHY and therefore entitled to DECIDE and to DO.

There are still those who CAN NOT INSIST, CAN NOT DEMAND, are not ABLE TO KNOW or to DO. They remain CHILDREN—without RIGHTS, without CHOICE, without FREEDOM, inhibited from pursuing HAPPINESS as they might wish to. Since they DO NOT KNOW, they CAN NOT DO and they NEED to be CARED FOR . . . without the ABILITY TO DECIDE, they CAN NOT DECIDE and therefore SHOULD NOT DECIDE. Their FUTURE is in the hands of those who DO KNOW, who CAN DECIDE, who TAKE CARE of them. The question remains as painful, as perplexing as ever: EXACTLY which INDIVIDUAL

PEOPLE are ENTITLED to LIVE LIFE FREELY PURSUING HAPPINESS as EQUALS of other MEN?

The history of AMERICA is the Story of EXACTLY who HAS the RIGHT to DECIDE EXACTLY who HAS the RIGHT to DECIDE.

Afterword

Let me tell you a story about why I chose to write about storytelling and especially why I chose to write about different kinds of people telling different kinds of stories.

When I was little, seven or eight and later, and people would ask me what I was (a common question back then; I don't know if it is still routine to ask kids what they are and expect Chinese or Scottish or half-British/half-French for an answer), anyway, when they'd ask I would say, "half-Italian Catholic, half-Hungarian Jew and one hundred percent American."

Neither side of my family considered themselves "American" when I was growing up. Americans were another kind of people categorized by my mother as cold, pleasure-loving, and unwilling to give you enough to eat when you went to their houses. For my father, Americans were hopelessly naive about the nature of the world; that a drinking country had voted in Prohibition always struck him as the last word in inconsistency and self-deception. Americans were also totally devoid of taste and likely to tell you an off-color joke, ask you if you'd ever been to a baseball game, and invite you for Thanksgiving dinner. My father waxed enthusiastic about Yankee ingenuity, however, and loved to be surprised by them acting like people. My mother always seemed rather disappointed that they acted like people. She was basically afraid of and intimidated by them, I think, and preferred them to be cold and unwilling to be truly generous. For my father the epitome of Americans being American was "the fake grandmother": a grandmother who charges her children to babysit for her grandchildren. For my mother what distinguished Americans from people is that they take vacations and spend money on themselves.

And I claimed to be 100 percent American, whatever that means. I took the melting pot seriously and personally. Here I was, born in the U.S. of two culturally ill-sorted people in an America which really seemed to be the land of possibilities of an otherwise impossible kind. Upward mobility? I'd seen it. My mother worked in the garment district and worked her way up to owning her own shop. She left it all to marry my father, an Intellectual. (It didn't work, but that's another story.) The land of opportunity? Certainly more than Europe at that time (early 1950's). Freedom? Those were the days of McCarthy, who was a real figure to me and dark muttery stories were heard that seemed very frightening and foreboding. But compared to the stories of gas chambers and concentration camps it just didn't seem that bad. Before I was born an American passport had been about the best guarantee of safety there was, and I felt inordinately glad from earliest childhood (three or four) that I was an American and I could get an American passport and cross borders without being afraid.

I knew a lot of Americans, too, of course. I went to a totally American school, meaning that there were no Catholics or Jews in it. It was a private girls school of genteel and Anglican persuasion. We sang "Holy, Holy, Holy," as far as I could see, at the drop of a hat and were expected to jump up from our seats when an adult entered the room and say "good morning Mrs. so and so" in happy unison. There was always some confusion when the janitor came in about whether you were supposed to stand up or not. I knew you weren't supposed to because I knew about those things. It seemed like the richer the girls were, the dumber. When I would go and visit my mother's relatives in New York, the teachers would say that I'd been with the Wop relatives again, but when my father would come to school they always seemed a bit bewildered. He intimidated them and they thought they owned the world. We had no money to speak of at home when I was growing up. My parents were separated and there never seemed to be much to go around. So, my mother took up babysitting. She babysat for the same type of people I went to school with, but she drew the line at sitting for anyone who actually was at the school. Next door, maybe. I went with her. We would go by taxi to some big empty house somewhere and look after the children. As far as I can remember, the children were all blond with skinny legs and limited intelligence. By the time my mother started sitting I was about ten or eleven, and so most of the children were younger than I was, but stupid. . . they were so incredibly limited that I couldn't believe it. I resented the babysitting because I would run out of books to read and these rich people, as my mother called them, didn't have any books. They always lived out in some wretched suburb, too, where there weren't any libraries. But they did have freezers which could keep ice cream and a TV which could get NBC, both lacking and lamented by my mother and myself in our own home. So we would watch TV and eat ice cream after the kids had been put to bed and wait up until some drunk Americans would come home at two or three o'clock in the morning smelling of alcohol and the outside world, then I'd get my books together and find my homework papers while the man couldn't find his checkbook, and the woman rushed off to bed because she was very tired. And then we'd leave, sometimes in a Mercedes, and sometimes in a filthy taxicab driven usually by Ernie who was a bookie and played the horses and made remarks and was a real person. He may have been Italian or Polish.

So there was all that, and it did not upset me particularly, but it did fascinate me. I never really wondered who was right about anything, they were all so sure that they were right. There was no other way to be or think or see the world my father's every word would say, and likewise my mother's and the school's and the drunken stockbroker's. There was only one world, I could see that, but a thousand views of it. Each view coherent, self-consistent, limiting in some respects, a blessed relief in others. Each existing like a self-satisfied planet revolving around a central star blissfully unaware of who was the center and who the wanderer.

It was a funny way to grow up. Never really socialized, never really a part, never minding not being a part except of course of the best clique at school, taking as truth somehow the best people felt about themselves and the worst anyone else said. I learned to listen very very hard to what people said and what different people said about the same things and I learned that the same facts, the same incidents, the same world was very very different when talked about by different people. The stories, the myths, the anecdotes were different. There was no truth, ever, in my world. Only stories, talk about the truth.

And yet people talked to each other and groups of similar people told similar stories and seemed to accept the versions of people like themselves without any difficulty. My mother and my teacher might see the same incident and talk about it very very differently. However, my mother and her sisters and the woman upstairs would report the same incident the same way, expressing surprise and outrage and relief at all the right points. And the teacher could talk to the other teachers and the WASP American parents and tell them a story which they understood. And I began to learn about which stories to tell to which people and that when you tell a story it is not the events which matter; it's the point which matters. The point says "hey, you and I know the world is like this and so this behavior, this event means this."

And so this book grows out of this story in lots of ways. First, this is a book about stories and about finding out what people are really talking about in their stories. It is based on the idea that stories are rooted in what you know to be true and that telling a story to someone who does not share your presuppositions about the world as expressed in that story means that he will not really know what you are talking about or care. When you talk to people who can't understand you, your story gets lost and what happens is that the people you are talking to know you are not one of them. They might put you in some sort of category and say that they never understand the stories Jews tell, but, more likely, they just feel bored and confused.

But I am left with the idea of whether there is an American story, since I just told you a story about different groups in the United States all talking at cross purposes and thinking the others were beyond the pale, if not downright immoral. I think that there is a core of common concerns among Americans, and who should be considered an American involves all those people who consider themselves to be American. Neither of my parents considered themselves American because they knew that they did not share the values of a lot of people whom they categorized as Americans, but those people who consider themselves Americans do share a set of values. Americans would find my father's insistence on taste and understanding the complexities of the political and economic world overly intellectual and elitist, and my mother's constant self-sacrifice at the cost of her own happiness to be far from reasonable, pathetic, maybe, even if in some sense commendable. And I share those values of those people who call themselves Americans. I believe deep down in *choices*, in the *ability* of the *individual* to *control* his own life in many ways, in the *responsibility* of the *individual* to make his own decisions. Furthermore, I can be moved by arguments that something is *not fair*. I think everyone should have *equal opportunities* and that different people have a *right* to *live their lives their own way as long as they don't hurt anybody else* because somehow people are all equal and have the right to choose what they want out of life and shouldn't be stopped from getting it through *accidents of birth* which they can't *control*. As long as an *individual* is competent he has the *right* to do what he thinks best and rise as high as he can rise. And all the rest.

I believe that *individuals* have *rights* and they have the *power* and the *responsibility* to make *decisions* for themselves. Furthermore, I believe that *time* is sequential, that events have *causes* which are to be found in either the *facts* of the natural world or in past events. I believe that it is possible to *understand* something and to *explain* it and I have almost a religious belief in the *power* of language to *facilitate change*. If you can talk about something you feel, then you will feel better. If you can *understand* a *problem*, you can *solve* it.

If you are an American, these may seem so stupidly trite that you would wonder why anyone would put these things down. You may think that you don't really think they are true. Perhaps some aren't for you. But I would bet that when you argue against one of them, it will be in terms of another. I've never met an American yet who doesn't believe that the individual is the central figure on the stage of the world and even arguments for being unselfish put forward by ten year olds involve being altruistic because even though it helps society, being unselfish makes you feel good and therefore is good for you.

For example, several people I know wrote down their versions of the story "The Boy Who Cried Wolf." In discussing the stories, it turned out that there were differences of opinion about what the story was really about, what the boy had done which meant he had to be punished. One opinion held by a couple of people was that the boy had been irresponsible to his sheep in crying wolf, and, in general, was a bad worker and irresponsible in carrying out his job. I felt that he made the villagers feel like such fools that they were embarrassed to look at each other and so he had disturbed the life of the village in that he disrupted social relations. Though our versions appeared totally odd to each other, there was nothing in the "responsibility" version which I could not understand, though I was surprised at what they thought the story was about (and indeed, in the stories, different aspects of the events and situations were emphasized by different people). They thought it was odd that I should be so concerned with the feelings of the villagers, but that people have feelings and that feelings are important considerations which one can tell a story about was certainly clear to them. That is the level of commonality I think there is among Americans and which defines American culture.

I'm not alone in this belief that American culture exists. It is a *commonsense* widely accepted belief. We can read about it, hear about it on television, talk about it to one another, discuss whether so- and-so is typically American and feel ourselves to be incredibly typical Americans when we go abroad as we find out that the world is inhabited by people who are really much more different from ourselves than we are from each other. Even when we feel more at home in some other country or with some other group we are expressing a rather American idea. Lots of people in all parts of the world are not interested in getting to know how the rest of the world is and would be appalled at the notion that one could possibly feel "at home" somewhere other than where home "is." In other words, Americans really locate their terms of reference inside themselves as individuals more than many other peoples do. It is not the place nor the others which determine our happiness, but our own experiences of those situations, what we make of them. This Apologia, Afterword, this piece of self-indulgent rhetoric, or whatever, is also American.

Think for a minute about the American psychotherapies which have grown up in the last twenty years or so. What do they emphasize? *Communication*, the *here and now*, the *freeing* of the *individual* from the *past* and from ties with family and loved ones which are not *appropriate* anymore. That *relationships* are transitory and should be *held onto* and *worked* for just as long as they have *meaning* in the *individual's* life, and that life moves in *time* and the *individual changes* as *time* moves by. Even more central to why this writing should be seen as American is that it is a confession of why I am involved with my subject, what it means to me. This usually has no place in academia, in science, in professional life.

Yet, one is always, inescapably, part of one's work. There is no objectivity, no outside, no place to run to hide one's personal, social, and cultural involvement in what one is doing. What reasons one gives will differ enormously depending on what one can count as a reason in one's world. The form in which one gives that answer will also depend on what can count as a way of presenting a reason. I believe in the *individual*, doing work *honestly* according to his own definition of honesty. And so I present a personal, intuitive, subjective account of the wellsprings of my work in the historical and psychological terms which make sense to me to clothe it in. And why? Because I would like to be able to be objective and I am apologizing because my work is not objective. But I hope by being *open* and *honest* about that lack of objectivity, that the work can be judged, not as a work of a traditional science, but as a work of a new science. A science which accepts that the observer is constrained by his system of observing as much as the observed are constrained and that one cannot understand an observation without understanding in some way what that observation means to the observer. If we do not know that, we do not have enough information about the observations to make them truly interpretable: we will not, therefore, be able to really understand the point of the story being told.

Bibliography

Barth, Fredrik. 1975. *Ritual and Knowledge Among the Baktaman of New Guinea*. New Haven: Yale University Press.

Benedict, Ruth. 1967. *The Chrysanthemum and the Sword*. New York: World Publishing Corp.

Brown, Penelope & Stephen Levinson. 1978. "Universals in Language Usage: Politeness Phenomena," in *Questions and Politeness Strategies in Social Interaction*, Esther N. Goody (ed.) 56-289. Cambridge: Cambridge University Press.

Colson, Elizabeth. 1971. "Heroism, Martyrdom, and Courage: An Essay on Tonga Ethics," in *The Translation of Culture: Essays to E. E. Evans-Pritchard*, T. O. Beidelman (ed.) 19-35. London: Tavistock Publications.

Dowty, David R. 1986. *The Effects of Aspectual Class on Temporal Structure of Discourse: Semantics or Pragmatics?* 37-61. D. Reidel Publishing Co..

Eisner, Janet. 1975. *A Grammar of Oral Narrative*. Unpublished University of Michigan Dissertation.

Emery, Stewart with Neal Rogin. 1978. Actualizations: *You Don't Have to Rehearse to Be Yourself*. Garden City, NY: Doubleday & Co., Dolphin Books.

Goffman, Erving. 1961. *Asylums: Essays on the Social Situation of Mental Patients and Other Inmates*. Garden City, NY: Anchor Books.

————. 1967. *Interaction Ritual: Essays on Face to Face Behavior*. Garden City, New York: Doubleday & Co., Inc.

Greenwald, Dr. Jerry A. 1975. *Creative Intimacy: How to Break the Patterns That Poison Your Relationships*. New York: Simon and Schuster.

Grimes, Joseph. 1982. "Topics within Topics," in *Analyzing Discourse: Text and Talk*. D. Tannen (ed.) 164-176. Washington, DC.: Georgetown University Press.

Gülich, Elisabeth. 1970. *Makrosyntax der Gliederungssignale im Gesprochenen Französisch*. München: Fink Verlag.

Hinrichs, E. "Temporal Anaphora in Discourse of English," *Linguistics and Philosophy* 9 (1), 63-82.

Hopper, Paul & Sandra Thompson. 1980. "Transitivity in Grammar and Discourse," *Language* 56 (2), 251-99.

Huges, Richard. 1944. *The Innocent Voyage. (AHigh Wind in Jamaica).* New York: Limited Editions Club.

Jefferson, Gail. 1979. "Sequential Aspects of Storytelling in Conversation," in *Studies in the Organization of Conversational Interaction*, J. Schenkein, (ed.) 219-248. New York: Academic Press.

Jones, Larry & Linda K. Jones. 1979. "Multiple Levels of Information in Discourse," in *Discourse Studies in Meso-American Languages: Volume 1*, Linda K. Jones (ed.) 3-28. Arlington, TX: Summer Institute of Linguistics.

Joos, Martin. 1968. *The English Verb: Form and Meaning.* Madison, WI: University of Wisconsin Press.

Kamp, H. & C. Rohrer. 1982. *Tense in Text.* Unpublished manuscript.

Labov, William. 1972. *Language in the Inner City: Studies in the Black English Vernacular = Conduct and Communication No. 3*, 354-396. Philadelphia: University of Pennsylvania Press.

————, and Joshua Waletzky. 1967. "Narrative Analysis: Oral Versions of Personal Experience," in *Essays on the Verbal and Visual Arts*, June Helms, (ed.) 12-44. Seattle: University of Washington press.

Longacre, Robert E. 1976. *An Anatomy of Speech Notions.* Lisse: The Peter de Ridder Press.

Lotman, Juri M. 1975. "On the Metalanguage of a Typological Description of Culture," *Semiotica 14*, 97-123.

Nerbonne, J. 1986. "Reference Time and Tense in Narrative," *Linguistics and Philosophy 9* (1), 83-96.

Newman, Mildred & Bernard Berkowitz. 1978. *How to Take Charge of Your Life.* New York: Bantam Books.

Polanyi-Bowditch, Livia. 1976a. "Why the Whats are When: Mutually Contextualized Realms of Narrative," in *Proceedings of the Second Annual Meeting of the Berkeley Linguistics Society*, February 14-16, 1976. K. Whistler, et. al (eds.) 59-78. Berkeley, CA: Berkeley Linguistics Society.

Polanyi, Livia. 1978a. *The American Story: Cultural Constraints on the Meaning and Structure of Stories in Conversation.* Unpublished Dissertation. University of Michigan.

————. 1978b. "So What's the Point?" *Semiotica*, 25 (3-4), 208-24.

————. 1981. "What Stories Can Tell Us About their Teller's World." *Poetics Today 2* (2), 97-112.

————. 1987. "Keeping it all Straight: Interpreting Narrative Time in Real Discourse," in *Proceedings of the West Coast Conference on Formal Linguistics: Volume 6*. M. Crowhurst (ed.) 229-247. Stanford: The Stanford Linguistics Association.

———— & Paul Hopper. forthcoming. "Reconsidering the Foreground Background Distinction," in *Text World, Text Perspective*, Jozsef Andor (ed.). Hamburg: Buske.

Putney, Snell & Gail J. Putney. 1972. *The Adjusted American: Normal Neuroses in the Individual and Society.* New York: Harper & Row, Perennial Library.

Rubin, Theodore Isaac. 1967. *The Winner's Notebook.* New York: Collier Books.

Sacks, Harvey. 1972. "On the Analyzability of Stories by Children," in *Directions in Sociolinguistics: The Ethnography of Communication,* John J. Gumperz and Dell Hymes (ed.) 325-45. New York: Holt, Rinehart and Winston.

———. 1974. "An Analysis in the Course of a Joke's Telling in Conversation," in *Explorations in the Ethnography of Speaking,* Richard Bauman and Joel Sherzer (eds.) 337-53. London: Cambridge University Press.

———. "Lecture Notes: Stories in Conversation." University of California. Spring, 1970 and Fall, 1971. Mimeo.

——— & Emanuel A. Schegloff. 1974. "Opening up Closings," in Roy Turner (ed.) 233-254. *Ethnomethodology.* Penguin Books.

———, Emanuel A. Schegloff, & Gail Jefferson. 1974. "A Simplest Systematics for the Organization of Turn-Taking for Conversation." *Language 50,* 696-735.

Schank, Roger & Robert Abelson. 1977. *Scripts, Plans, Goals and Understanding.* Hillsdale, NJ: Lawrence Erlbaum Associates.

Schegloff, Emanuel A. 1971. "Notes on Conversational Practice Formulating Place," in *Language and Social Context,* Giglioli (ed.). Penguin Books.

Schiffrin, Deborah. 1982. *Discourse Markers: A Semantic Resource for the Construction of Conversation.* Unpublished University of Pennsylvania Ph. D. Dissertation.

Tannen, Deborah. 1984. *Conversational Style: Analyzing Talk among Friends.* Norwood, NJ: Ablex Publishing Corp.

van Dijk, T. A. (Ed). In press. *The Handbook of Discourse Analysis.* New York: Academic press.

Vendler, Z. 1967. *Linguistics and Philosophy.* Ithaca, NY: Cornell University Press.

Wilensky, Robert. 1978. *Understanding Goal Based Stories.* (Tech Report 140). New Haven: Yale University Computer Science.

Author Index

Subject Index

A

Acceptability of stories, 1
Acting out as evaluative device, 92
Adequate Paraphrase, 26
  "Baddest girl in the
    neighboorhood," 38, 141
  "Eating on the N. Y.
    Thruway," 59, 131
  how to construct, 27-30
  "The Ordeal," 144
  reported speech in, 28
  "The Robbery," 149
Adult
  always in control, 115, 116, 147
  competent,116-117, 193
  MANQUÉ, 186
  strength of, 117
  trusts only himself,116
ADULTS 153-157, 160
  "Eating on the New York
    Thruway," 138
  KNOWLEDGE, 153
  nature of, 131, 138-139, 147-148,
    153-154, 167
  pain, 146
  PROPERTIES OF, 149, 175-179,
    181
  RESPONSIBILITIES OF, 175-
    176, 177-178
  WANTS OF, 177
Aesthetics, 127
Alienation, 133, 136
Aloneness of individual, 119, 133,
  139
Altered perceptions, 126
Ambiguity in oral storytelling, 45
Ambition, 113

American cultural constructs,
  grammar of, 3,, 109-114, 151-179
American-heterogenerity, 12-14
  values, 13
American psychotherapy, 120
American world view, 109-194
Americanness of author, 4, 114, 195-
  202
"Americans," 12-14
Amplification, 79-80
Anger, 136
Appropriate stories, 25-26
Autism, 124
Autonomy, 128, 134

B

"Baddest girl in the
  Neighborhood," 30, 44
  chart of evaluation, 35-36
  courage in, 38
  cultural constructs in mainline
    story, 141-143
  discussion of evaluation in, 35-38
  durative-descriptive
    propositions in, 34-35
  event, clauses in, 32, 33, 37
  event propostitions in, 33-34
  non-storyworld, clauses in, 32-33
  standing up for rights in, 37, 143
  teller of, 12
  text of, 31-32
Basic human needs, 117, 118, 127
Bigoted, 103
Best friends, 132
"But," 27